LIN
BY LINE

The West Coast Main Line
London Euston to Glasgow Central

MARTIN BUCK

&

MARK RAWLINSON

*Freightmaster
Publishing*

CONTENTS

INTRODUCTION.   3

W.C.M.L. ~ A Brief History   4

USING THIS BOOK.   8

EUSTON - RUGBY.   9
RUGBY - PRESTON 33
PRESTON - CARLISLE. 67
CARLISLE - GLASGOW 91

GALLERY. 117

NORTHAMPTON LOOP 133

GLOSSARY :   Miles & Chains 144
                 Photographers. 148
                 Bibliography 148

Schematic Maps & Research	:	Mark Rawlinson
e-mail	:	mark.rawlinson@virgin.net
fax	:	01524-730591
Layout, Text & Captions	:	Martin Buck
e-mail	:	martin.buck1@virgin.net
fax	:	01793-644079
ISBN	:	0-9537540-0-6
Published by	:	Freightmaster Publishing
		158 Overbrook
		SWINDON SN3 6AY
Printed by	:	Tekprint Ltd., SWINDON

INTRODUCTION

THANK YOU for buying this copy of LINE BY LINE, a completely new concept in the world of railway books!

THE IDEA behind this book stems from a pet hate - to find out about a particular railway route in this country, whether for reference or photographic purposes, one has to refer to many books, most of which are now out of print.

There has never before been a single title which includes full details of:

- Gradient Profiles and Topography   - Miles and Chains
- Running Lines, Crossovers & Junctions   - Station Layouts
- Tunnels and Viaducts   - Sites of Closed Stations and watertroughs
- Signalboxes and their area of control   - Photographic Opportunities

Well, following 18 months of painstaking research and work, not only does such a book now exist, but it is fully illustrated too!

DEVELOPING into a comprehensive series, each edition of LINE BY LINE will feature a major railway route, plotting its course schematically and highlighting all the aspects listed above along the way. Up to date photographs, submitted by prominent contemporary photographers, will illustrate not just the route but also the range of motive power and types of train to be seen on it.

THIS EDITION covers the West Coast Main Line (WCML). Our journey begins at Euston station, London, from where the route is traced northwards in five-mile sections until we reach Glasgow Central over 400 miles (and 148 pages of maps and photographs) later. The Northampton Loop is also featured as, in effect, it represents the 'slow' lines between Roade and Rugby.

EVERY five mile section is accompanied by at least one photograph so, unlike previous books featuring the WCML which 'cherry pick' the best locations, all parts of the route are featured, however featureless they may be. To make the book as up to date as possible, the pictorial content has been restricted to photographs taken since 1990.

In addition, there is a special "Gallery" section, featuring 24 high calibre colour photographs of the classic Shap and Beattock areas, plus full-colour reproductions of Ordnance Survey Landranger maps clearly marked with the location of each shot.

FINALLY we would like to extend our thanks to the photographers listed in the Glossary, who have kindly allowed us to use their excellent material, most of which has never been published before.

                                                                                    MB / MR

The W.C.M.L. ~ A brief history

Background:

This edition of LINE BY LINE cannot be, and does not lay any claim to be, the definitive article on the WCML; but it is a practical guide to the route as it is today, in words and pictures.

However, any title needs a slice of history to provide a sense of perspective and so, to set the scene for this brief narrative, our history lesson is confined to dealing with the WCML as a fully electrified route.

The 1955 Modernisation Plan instigated the AC electric system from Manchester and Liverpool to London. By 1964 electrification had only reached Rugby, necessitating a changeover to diesel traction, and not until 1966 did through electric-hauled services reach Euston. In 1969, a £30M upgrade was authorised by the Government between Weaver Junction and Glasgow and a year later full electrification was given the go-ahead. From May 1974, full West Coast electric timetabled services came into force.

The upgrade of the WCML in the 1970s represented a major challenge to engineers in order to cater for the overhead catenary. Over 300 bridges had to be restructured and in some cases the track had to be realigned and lowered to overcome hurdles like, for example, where the WCML passed under the canal at Preston Brook.

Resignalling also resulted in major developments with new signalling centres at Warrington, Preston, Carlisle and Motherwell - with the existing one at Glasgow Central being upgraded with new equipment. These replaced a total of 179 mechanical signalboxes; 91 of them in the Motherwell/Glasgow area alone and, when commissioned, Motherwell's panel covered one of the largest areas in the world.

As for motive power, a variety of diesel and electric locomotives have worked passenger and freight turns on the WCML. Some 30 years ago, pairs of Class 50s could be seen working Anglo-Scottish expresses between Crewe and Glasgow and now electric traction remains the staple motive power. Relatively new Class 92 electric locomotives now work heavy freights unassisted over the northern stretches of the route.

As to the future - an upgrade of the WCML is underway to allow for new trains and faster services. Engineering work is being undertaken to simplify the track layout between London Euston and Camden as well as Euston station itself being remodelled. Proposals are also being considered to develop flyovers and track rationalisation at many locations to ease congestion; of which, Hanslope Junction and Nuneaton are possible candidates.

Virgin Trains, who currently operate West Coast passenger services, plan to introduce Advanced Tilting Trains (ATTs) for West Coast services commencing early in the new Millennium; somewhat ironic in view of the now infamous Advanced Passenger Train (APT), which despite trials between 1984-87, failed to come to fruition!

The Route itself:

Euston to Rugby: The exit from London Euston is a stiff climb of 1 in 70/112/77 to Camden after which the WCML reaches Willesden; a major junction for freight services travelling to the former Western, Southern and Eastern Regions. There is also a plethora of interest here as the electric locomotive depot, Intermodal and Post Office 'Railnet' terminals are all within close proximity.

The suburban "D.C. lines" to Watford leave Euston as well as the WCML; the Bakerloo underground line shares the same track until Harrow & Wealdstone. Four track running lines continue between Euston and Roade, where the up & down slow lines leave for Northampton before rejoining the main line at Rugby.

The Grand Union Canal skirts the WCML between Abbots Langley and Tring and at Watford gap the line runs parallel to the M1 motorway; Kilsby Tunnel, at 1m. 666yds, represents the longest tunnel on the entire route.

At Rugby, the lines serving Birmingham and the West Midlands leave the WCML and marks the site of the former AEI works and Testing Station for the early Class 81-85 electric locomotives.

Rugby to Preston : The WCML continues through the Trent Valley, passing Tamworth and Lichfield with their low & high level stations until Colwich, the first junction for Stoke and Manchester. The lines serving Birmingham & the West Midlands trail in and rejoin the WCML at Stafford No.4 junction.

After Stafford, famous for its impressive manual frame signalboxes, the WCML reaches Basford Hall yard, Crewe, which exists primarily to re-marshall Freightliner services. Most freight trains use the 'Independent Lines' to avoid Crewe station, linking up again with the WCML at Coal Yard Junction. The station itself was extensively re-modelled during 1984/85 and remains the junction for North Wales.

At Weaver Junction the mainline for Liverpool leaves the WCML. After crossing the Manchester Ship Canal at Acton Grange Junction, where the Chester lines join the WCML, the mainline sweeps round an embankment to reach Warrington Bank Quay station, whilst two lines drop down into Arpley freight yard.

Ostensibly, the running lines are double track between Crewe and Glasgow although sections of four track exist when other routes join and leave the WCML. For example, from Acton Grange until Winwick Junction, when the Earlstown spur disappears, and from Golborne Junction after the Parkside lines have trailed in. Of note, is the switch to local mileage/mileposts northward from Golborne Junction.

The early '70s modernisation programme resulted in extensive track rationalisation in the Wigan area and the elimination of some junctions, such as Boars Head and Standish. The lines leading to the 'Settle & Carlisle' diversionary route leave the WCML at Farington, just south of Preston - Preston itself being an important interchange for Blackpool and the Lancashire mill towns of Blackburn and Burnley.

Preston to Carlisle : At Hest Bank, the WCML reaches its lowest level and the closest it gets to its namesake by Morecambe Bay. From Carnforth, with no WCML platforms and the junction for the ex-Furness Railway to Barrow, the WCML climbs 31 miles to 916ft. at Shap summit and then sees this height fall away over the same distance to Carlisle.

Beforehand, the route climbs at grades as steep as 1in 104 to Grayrigg and, in steam days, enginemen had to decide whether to stop at Tebay to pick up a 'banking' engine for the final push to Shap summit. Of course, whilst downhill from here, the route is an equally gruelling climb southwards from Carlisle.

The Border city of Carlisle was a confluence of major railway companies: the Caledonian, Glasgow & South Western, London North Western, Midland, North British and the North Eastern Railway. Carlisle Citadel station is impressive for its architecture and screenwalls which originally supported an overall roof spanning almost six acres.

There used to be a goods-avoiding line between Upperby Junction and Caldew Junction until 1st May 1984, when a section of a Liverpool - Glasgow freightliner broke away. A major disaster was avoided at the station, by a signalman switching the runaways onto the goods line. At speeds close to 70mph passing Rome Street Junction, the runaways left the track, careering into the River Caldew taking part of the bridge with them.

Carlisle to Glasgow : The ex-Caledonian route passes Carlisle Kingmoor depot/yard and breaches the Anglo-Scottish border at Gretna. The WCML proceeds to Beattock where a Class 20 diesel, manned by Carstairs crew, used to be stabled for 'banking' duties. A ten mile ascent then ensues mostly at a ruling gradient of 1 in 75 or thereabouts before Beattock Summit is reached some 1,016 ft. above sea level.

When electrification was switched on, power was provided by the South of Scotland Electricity Board, fed into four feeder stations. Of particular interest, was that the one at Ecclefechan was fed by a direct power line from the nuclear power station at Chapelcross whilst, at Elvanfoot, the supply was derived from the 275kV grid for the first time ever.

At Carstairs, major track alterations took place in the 1970s to allow line speeds to rise from 50 to 90mph. Of note, the up main line through the station was lifted 21 inches and the platform had to be raised to match, with steps/ramps down to the station buildings. Locomotive changes to diesel traction were a regular occurrence at Carstairs until electrification through to Edinburgh was completed in March 1991.

The WCML drops steeply from Craigenhill Summit and at Motherwell, freight services leave for Mossend, where Coatbridge marks the limit of electrification on this line. After passing Polmadie, a principal servicing depot for rolling stock, the WCML finally crosses the multi-track bridge spanning the River Clyde into Glasgow Central - 401.35 miles from London Euston and the end of the WEST COAST MAIN LINE.

Now turn the page and retrace the route in more detail, *LINE BY LINE*.

USING THIS BOOK

An Overview

In compiling this book, the West Coast Main Line from Euston to Glasgow has been split into five mile sections, with one section per page. Each section comprises of:

- A gradient profile
- A track plan
- A photograph

The Gradient Profiles

These show a 'cutaway' side-on view of the section, exaggerated enough to clearly show the changing gradients of the route. There is a vertical scale, marked in 200 foot increments. The lowest point of the line is at Hest Bank (sea level), while the highest (Beattock summit) bursts through the top of the page!

The Track Plans

These show a 'birds eye' view of the route, with running lines, junctions, etc. clearly marked. It cannot be stressed enough that these plans are schematic and, while the maps themselves are to scale, certain features have had to be slightly compressed to maintain clarity.

Key to Symbols

To make this book easy to use, cryptic symbols & abbreviations have been kept to the absolute minimum:

▬	=	station platform (in use)	*U.G.L.*	=	Up Goods Loop
▭	=	station platform (disused)	*D.G.L.*	=	Down Goods Loop
SB	=	signal box	*U.P.L.*	=	Up Passenger Loop
PSB	=	power signal box	*D.P.L.*	=	Down Passenger Loop
⋮	=	boundary between signal box areas			

The following pages depict the track layout of the WCML at the time of going to press (December 1999) - the sole exception is London Euston, which was in the process of being remodelled, so the revised layout as published by Railtrack in Summer 1999, is shown.

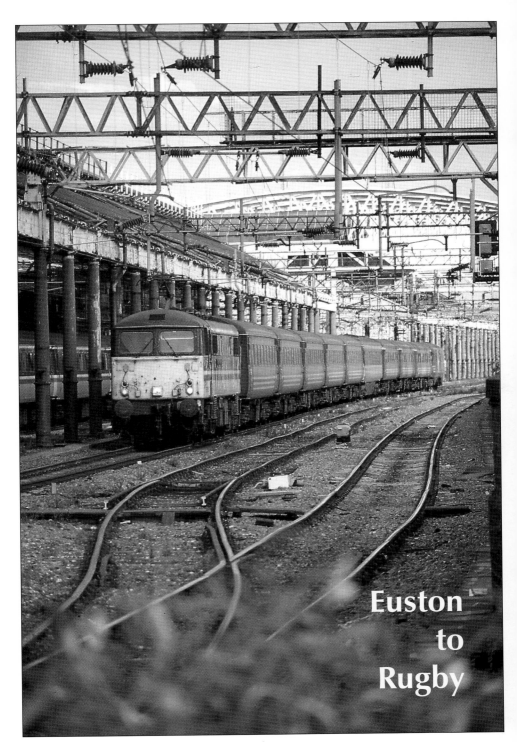

**Euston
to
Rugby**

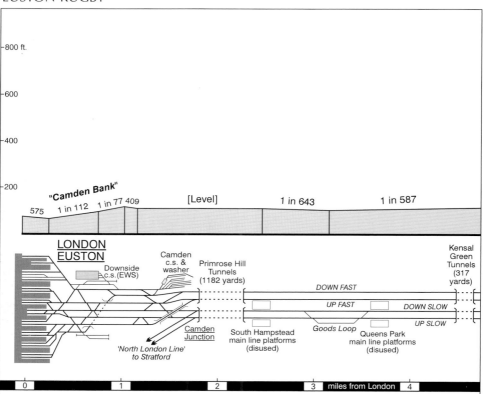

—800 ft.

—600

—400

—200

"Camden Bank"

575   1 in 112   1 in 77   409   [Level]   1 in 643   1 in 587

LONDON
EUSTON

Downside
c.s.(EWS)

Camden
c.s. &
washer

Primrose Hill
Tunnels
(1182 yards)

Kensal
Green
Tunnels
(317
yards)

DOWN FAST

UP FAST   DOWN SLOW

Goods Loop   UP SLOW

Camden
Junction

'North London Line'
to Stratford

South Hampstead
main line platforms
(disused)

Queens Park
main line platforms
(disused)

0   1   2   3   miles from London   4

EUSTON : The complex track in the foreground illustrates why a new, simpler, layout at Euston is required. A Class 87 No. 87020 *North Briton* propels the 1215 service from Birmingham New Street into the terminus and passes another Class 87, a Class 90 and a Class 313 unit in the process. (BM 3/99)

EUSTON DOWN CARRIAGE SIDINGS : The revamp of Euston has seen engineers trains running in and out of the station with infrastructure materials; one such journey saw Class 66 No. 66017 (above) haul a rake of MHA's past a Class 86 stabled outside Euston Down Carriage Sidings. (AG 12/98)

An aerial view depicts Class 87 No. 87002 *Royal Sovereign* (below) on an ECS stabled alongside the carriage sidings as a pair of Class 321/4 units head north on the 1004 Euston - Milton Keynes. (AG 12/98)

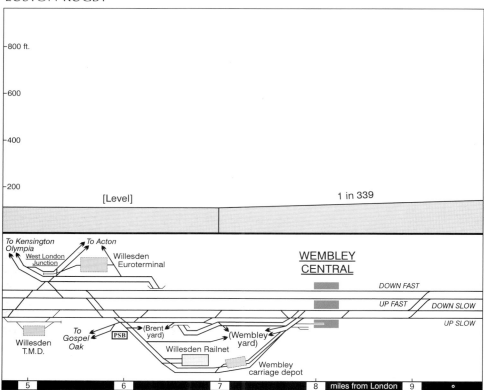

-800 ft.

-600

-400

-200

[Level]   1 in 339

To Kensington Olympia
To Acton
West London Junction
Willesden Euroterminal

WEMBLEY CENTRAL

DOWN FAST

UP FAST / DOWN SLOW

UP SLOW

Willesden T.M.D.
To Gospel Oak
PSB
(Brent yard)
Willesden Railnet
(Wembley yard)
Wembley carriage depot

5   6   7   8 miles from London 9

WILLESDEN : Travelling beneath Willesden High Level station is Class 321/4 No. 321407 on the 1031 local service from Milton Keynes to Euston. Trains ceased to stop at the Low Level main line station in 1962, after which the tracks were realigned and the platforms demolished as part of the 25kV electrification scheme. Note the staircase linking the two levels. (BM 1/95)

WEMBLEY YARD : Railfreight Distribution introduced 'Intermodal' services through the Channel Tunnel to Europe in June 1994. All traffic runs to/from Wembley yard, where containers from continental destinations are remarshalled into trains for domestic terminals. In Wembley yard holding sidings (above), locomotives await their next turn of duty, with Class 47s Nos. 47304 and 47218 *United Transport Europe* to the fore. (BM 4/97)

WILLESDEN RAILNET : The purpose built Royal Mail Distribution Centre at Willesden was commissioned in 1996. An interior view depicts two Class 325 EMUs Nos. 325007 and 325016 (below) in the spacious surroundings afforded for the loading/unloading of the nation's mail. (BM 3/97)

—800 ft.

—600

—400

1 in 339

—200

Willesden PSB ┊ Watford PSB

HARROW & WEALDSTONE

Hatch End
main line platforms
(disused)

DOWN FAST

UP FAST   *DOWN SLOW*

UP SLOW

10   11   12   13   miles from London   14

HARROW & WEALDSTONE : The up and down 'slow line' platforms are illustrated in this view of Harrow & Wealdstone station, where a 'Stanstead Skytrain' liveried Class 322 EMU No. 322482 is seen making its station stop with the 'Silverlink' 1035 Milton Keynes - Euston service. (BM 2/99)

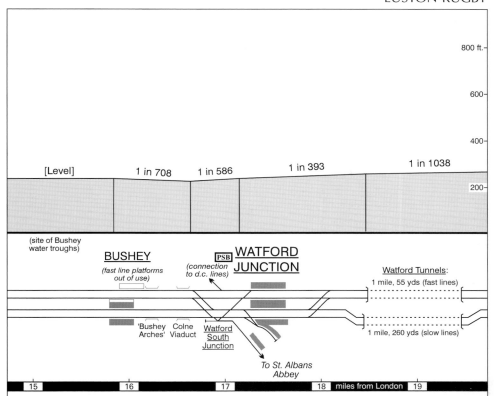

800 ft.
600
400
200

[Level]   1 in 708   1 in 586   1 in 393   1 in 1038

(site of Bushey
water troughs)

BUSHEY
*(fast line platforms
out of use)*

[PSB] **WATFORD
JUNCTION**
*(connection
to d.c. lines)*

Watford Tunnels:
1 mile, 55 yds (fast lines)

'Bushey   Colne
Arches' Viaduct

Watford
South
Junction

1 mile, 260 yds (slow lines)

To St. Albans
Abbey

15   16   17   18   miles from London   19

WATFORD JUNCTION : DVT No. 82105 leads 1A35, the 0945 Liverpool - Euston through Watford Junction and passes Class 313 No. 313006 berthed in the D.C. bay platforms. Watford Junction also sees a regular Class 313 -operated shuttle service to St Albans. (BB 2/99)

—800 ft.

—600

—400

1 in 508

1 in 335

—200

KINGS LANGLEY

APSLEY

HEMEL
HEMPSTEAD

Up Goods Loop

| 20 | 21 | 22 | 23 | miles from London | 24 |

HEMEL HEMPSTEAD : An unidentified Class 87 heads a down express past the rather stark and functional style of architecture which comprise the present day station buildings at Hemel Hempstead. To the back left of the picture, the old station building can be seen plus the short bay platform formerly used for mail traffic; the track having being lifted since this photograph was taken. (BB 2/99)

800 ft.
600
400
200

1 in 335

BERKHAMSTED

Northchurch
Tunnels
(349 yards)

DOWN FAST

DOWN SLOW   UP FAST

UP SLOW

25   26   27   28   miles from London   29

BERKHAMSTED : Although booked for a Class 90 locomotive, 1A52, the 1330 Manchester Piccadilly - Euston, speeds along the up fast at Berkhamstead with a Class 87 in charge. Note the rake is the 'wrong way round', in that the locomotive is leading and, unusually, the DVT (out of view) is at the 'country' end of the train. (BB 2/99)

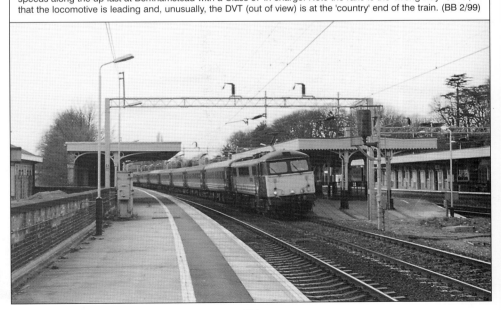

17

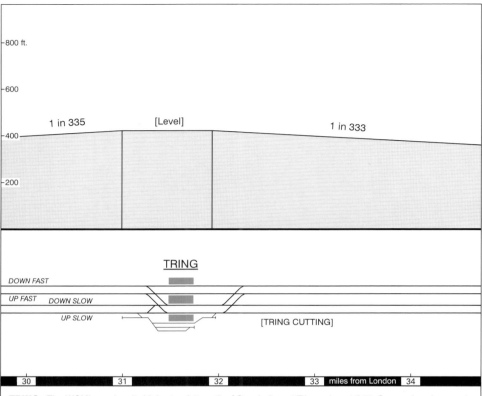

-800 ft.

-600

1 in 335   [Level]   1 in 333

-400

-200

TRING

DOWN FAST

UP FAST   DOWN SLOW

UP SLOW   [TRING CUTTING]

30   31   32   33   miles from London   34

TRING : The WCML reaches its highest point south of Oxenholme at Tring, where 5A90, Crewe - London empty mail units, headed by No. 325010, is seen passing through the station. Note the electronic platform route indicator and Tring Cutting visible in the background. (MB 6/99)

800 ft.

600

400

1 in 333

1 in 540   1 in 1330

200

Watford PSB : Bletchley PSB

CHEDDINGTON

Ledburn

Bridego Bridge,
site of the
Great Train Robbery
8th August 1963

| 35 | 36 | 37 | 38 | miles from London | 39 |

CHEDDINGTON : Class 66 No. 66101 hurries 4A36, Hams Hall - Wembley 'Intermodal' (the first train to be booked a Class 66 on the WCML) through Cheddington station. Just to the north of here at Sears Crossing on 8th August 1963, the up 'West Coast Postal' was stopped at a tampered red signal. Thieves overpowered both driver and second-man, uncoupled D326 and the first two vehicles, and forced them to drive to Bridego Bridge, where items valued in excess of £2½ million were stolen. (MB 6/99)

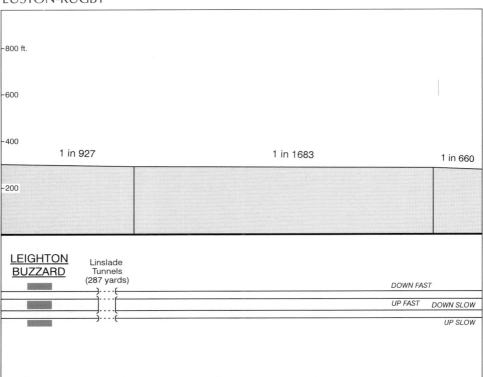

-800 ft.

-600

-400

1 in 927   1 in 1683   1 in 660

-200

LEIGHTON
BUZZARD
　Linslade
　Tunnels
　(287 yards)

DOWN FAST

UP FAST   DOWN SLOW

UP SLOW

40   41   42   43   miles from London   44

LEIGHTON BUZZARD : This photograph clearly illustrates that aesthetic buildings can be designed to cater for todays' rail user. The train featured is a Class 321 unit No. 321430 seen passing through the up slow platform with the 1330 Northampton - Euston. (BB 2/99)

LINSLADE TUNNEL : Connex Class 319/0 EMU No. 309010 bursts from the centre bore of Linslade Tunnel as it approaches Leighton Buzzard with the 1323 Rugby - Gatwick Airport service. (BM 2/99)

BLETCHLEY FLYOVER : The line from Bedford to Bicester/Oxford avoids the WCML by means of a flyover, visible in the background, as Class 90 No. 90009 *The Economist* propels 1A44, the 1145 Liverpool - Euston, through Bletchley station - the Power Signal Box is on the right. (BB 2/99)

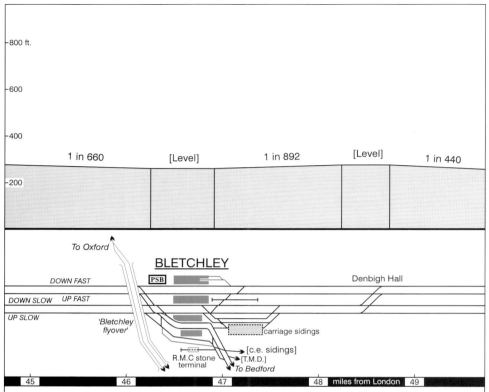

-800 ft.

-600

-400

| 1 in 660 | [Level] | 1 in 892 | [Level] | 1 in 440 |

-200

To Oxford

BLETCHLEY

DOWN FAST
PSB
Denbigh Hall

DOWN SLOW   UP FAST

UP SLOW

'Bletchley flyover'

carriage sidings

R.M.C stone terminal
[c.e. sidings]
[T.M.D.]
To Bedford

| 45 | 46 | 47 | 48 | miles from London | 49 |

BLETCHLEY : Class 58 No. 58021 awaits a path onto the up slow line at Bletchley station with a rake of MHA wagons bound for engineering work on the main line at Tring. The track to the right of the picture leads to the engineers sidings, TMD and the line to Bedford. (AG 4/98)

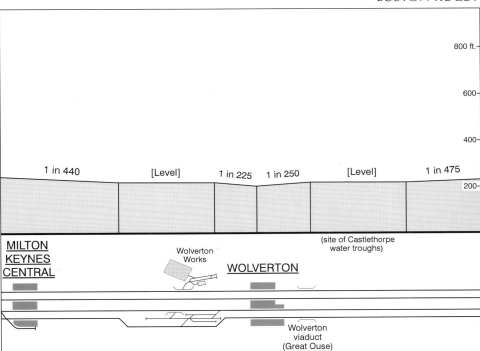

800 ft.-

600-

400-

1 in 440   [Level]   1 in 225   1 in 250   [Level]   1 in 475

200-

MILTON
KEYNES
CENTRAL

Wolverton
Works

WOLVERTON

(site of Castlethorpe
water troughs)

Wolverton
viaduct
(Great Ouse)

50   51   52   53   miles from London   54

WOLVERTON : A lightweight 4Z59, Ditton - Thamesport 'Intermodal', passes through Wolverton station on the up slow, headed by Class 47 No. 47286 *Port of Liverpool*. To the west of the station (out of view) is Wolverton Carriage works, home of the Royal Train. (MB 6/99)

23

MILTON KEYNES : The 'New Town' of Milton Keynes abounds in modern architecture. A stylish glass and steel office block looms over Class 60 No. 60061 *Alexander Graham Bell* (above) as it trundles along the up platform slow line heading 6B10, Peak Forest - Bletchley stone train. (KF 6/95)

An aerial view shows Class 87 No. 87027 *Wolf of Badenoch* (below) powering 1H07, the 0850 Euston - Manchester, calling at Milton Keynes Central at the same time as No. 87020 *North Briton* makes its stop on 1A21, the 0819 Wolverhampton - Euston. (AG 8/98)

CASTLETHORPE : Class 90 No. 90149 leads a well loaded 4L97, Trafford Park - Felixstowe freightliner on the up fast line at Castlethorpe, north of Wolverton. The water troughs used in steam days are long gone, although the redundant water tower still remains. (AG 8/98)

ASHTON : The shadows begin to lengthen behind Class 325 units Nos. 325003/325004 as they head away from the photographer on 1A89, Crewe - London mail. The location is the Northamptonshire/Buckinghamshire border near the village of Ashton. (AG 9/97)

800 ft.

600

400

1 in 326   1 in 410   1 in 330

200

Bletchley PSB : Rugby PSB

Fast Line
Platforms
still intact

Hanslope Junction   DOWN FAST

UP FAST   DOWN NORTHAMPTON

(site of
Castlethorpe
station,
closed 1964)

UP NORTHAMPTON   (site of
Roade
station,
closed
1964)

55   56   57   58   miles from London   59

ROADE : The site of Roade station is a very popular 'spotting' location, although it is rather disappointing from a photographic point of view. One of only a handful of freight trains not booked to travel via the Northampton Loop is 4L97, Trafford Park - Felixstowe freightliner, seen at Roade in the care of Class 90 No. 90143 *Freightliner Coatbridge*. (MB 6/99)

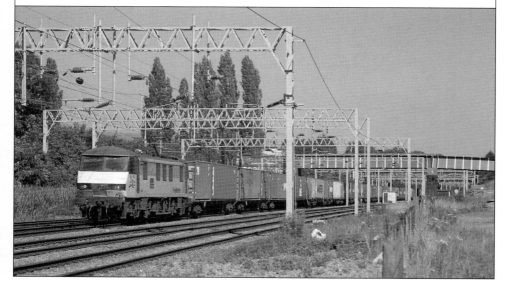

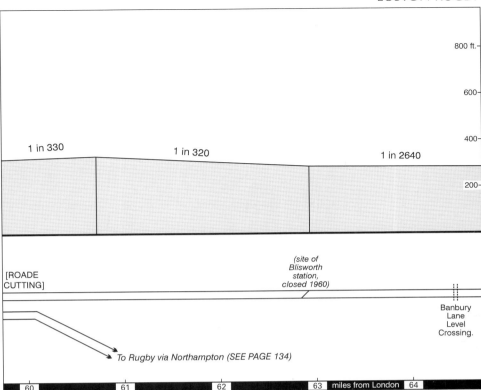

800 ft.

600

400

200

1 in 330

1 in 320

1 in 2640

[ROADE CUTTING]

(site of Blisworth station, closed 1960)

Banbury Lane Level Crossing.

To Rugby via Northampton (SEE PAGE 134)

| 60 | 61 | 62 | 63 | miles from London | 64 |

ROADE CUTTING : Roade cutting is unique as the fast and slow lines are at different levels. The lower level carries the 'Northampton Loop', which descends towards the Nene Valley at 1 in 200 and is encased in a metal cage. This view shows Class 90 No. 90007 in the cutting with a southbound ECS, formed of an ECML Class 91 locomotive and a rake of Mark 4 coaches. (AG 4/92)

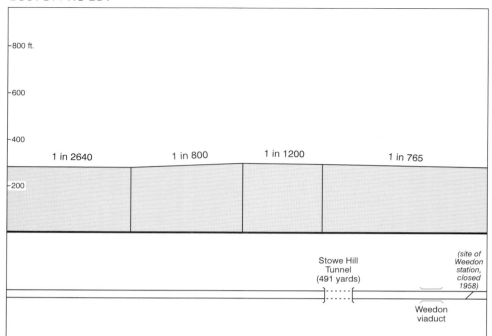

800 ft.

600

400

| 1 in 2640 | 1 in 800 | 1 in 1200 | 1 in 765 |

200

Stowe Hill
Tunnel
(491 yards)

(site of Weedon station, closed 1958)

Weedon
viaduct

| 65 | 66 | 67 | 68 | miles from London | 69 |

WEEDON : This particular stretch of the WCML abounds in locations which afford good photographic opportunities. Class 87 No. 87001 *Royal Scot* is seen at Weedon on a down express, made up of mark 3 air-conditioned stock; the north portal of Stowe Hill tunnel is visible in the background. (KF 3/98)

800 ft.

600

400

1 in 490

1 in 350

1 in 415

200

| 70 | 71 | 72 | 73 | miles from London | 74 |

WATFORD GAP : Class 90 No. 90005 races the traffic on the adjacent M1 motorway in charge of the 1310 Euston - Liverpool at 'Watford Gap'; so named because the A5 & M1 roads, the Grand Union Canal and the railway are all forced together through a small gap in the surrounding hills. (AG 2/94)

-800 ft.

-600

-400   1 in 415   1 in 640   [Level]   1 in 870

1 in 370

-200

Kilsby Tunnel
(1 mile, 656 yards)

(site of
Welton
station,
closed 1958)

75   76   77   78   miles from London   79

KILSBY TUNNEL : For the record, and by exception, a photograph of the ill-fated APT (No. 370007) emerging from the longest tunnel on the entire WCML at 1mile 656 yards long. (KF 7/82)

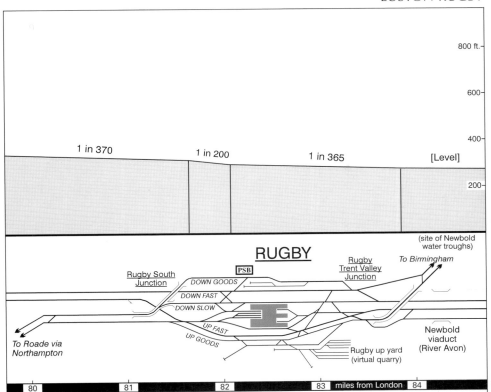

RUGBY

1 in 370	1 in 200	1 in 365	[Level]	

800 ft.
600
400
200

PSB

(site of Newbold water troughs)

To Birmingham

Rugby Trent Valley Junction

Rugby South Junction

DOWN GOODS
DOWN FAST
DOWN SLOW
UP FAST
UP GOODS

To Roade via Northampton

Newbold viaduct (River Avon)

Rugby up yard (virtual quarry)

80   81   82   83   miles from London   84

RUGBY SOUTH JUNCTION : The flora appears to overwhelm Class 90 No. 90137 as it negotiates the flyover at Rugby South Junction, having come off the Northampton Loop with 6K86, Wembley - Crewe 'Connectrail'. The distinctive masts of Rugby radio transmitter, from which clocks are set world-wide, dominate the sky. (AG 6/96)

RUGBY : Looking south, Class 47 No. 47786 *Roy Castle OBE* (above) speeds past Rugby Power Signalbox with the VSOE luxury train conveying punters from London Victoria to Liverpool for the 'Grand National'. Note the splendid metallic canopy spanning the station platforms. (AG 4/98)

On a test run, a Eurostar EMU set (below) with power car No. 3302 leading, heads past Rugby station on the down fast line en-route to Crewe. (KF 8/97)

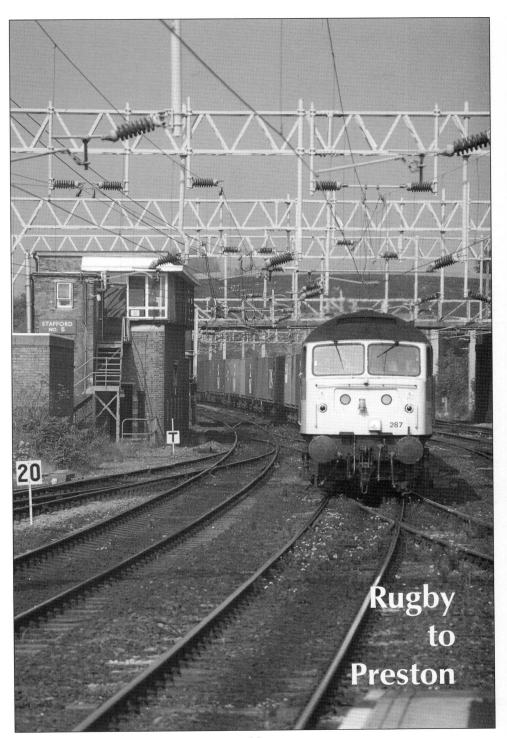

STAFFORD NO. 5

20

287

**Rugby
to
Preston**

-800 ft.

-600

-400

1 in 330   [Level]   1 in 510   1 in 395   1 in 600   1 in 530   [Level]

-200

Rugby PSB   Nuneaton PSB

DOWN FAST

UP FAST

UP SLOW

(site of Brinklow station, closed 1975)

Nettle Hill viaduct

85   86   87   88   miles from London   89

CATHIRON : Three running lines greet the photographer at Cathiron, a few miles into the Trent Valley. A Class 37, No. 37697, is seen crawling along the up slow line near to some old railway cottages, heading 7A74, Stud Farm – Rugby ballast train. (KF 4/97)

800 ft.

600

400

| [Level] | 1 in 330 | 1 in 1254 | 1 in 320 |

200

*(site of
Shilton
station,
closed 1957)*

*(site of
Bulkington
station,
closed 1931)*

DOWN FAST

UP FAST

UP SLOW

90   91   92   93 miles from London 94

NETTLE HILL : The WCML runs parallel to the Oxford Canal at Nettle Hill, where Class 86 No. 86426 *Pride of the Nation* is seen heading north with 5F94, Euston – Warrington empty mail vans. The M6 motorway is also visible in the background. (MB 6/99)

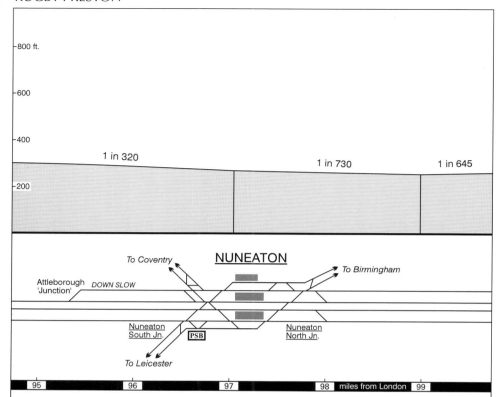

- 800 ft.
- 600
- 400
1 in 320   1 in 730   1 in 645
- 200

To Coventry   **NUNEATON**   To Birmingham
Attleborough DOWN SLOW
'Junction'
Nuneaton   Nuneaton
South Jn.   PSB   North Jn.
To Leicester

95   96   97   98 miles from London 99

NUNEATON : Class 31 No. 31272 sits at Nuneaton station with an engineers train; one of many locomotives to carry the distinctive 'Dutch' yellow and grey livery to denote allocation to engineering duties. Nuneaton being a crossover for trains running between the West Midlands and East Midlands/Anglia. (KF 9/93)

800 ft.

600

400

1 in 645   1 in 415   1 in 321

200

ATHERSTONE

DOWN SLOW

DOWN FAST

UP FAST

UP SLOW

| 100 | 101 | 102 | 103 | miles from London | 104 |

ATHERSTONE : Atherstone station is unremarkable except for the fine architecture of the station building, seen prominently in this picture behind Class 153 unit No. 153365 working the 1219 Stafford – Nuneaton. (KF 3/97)

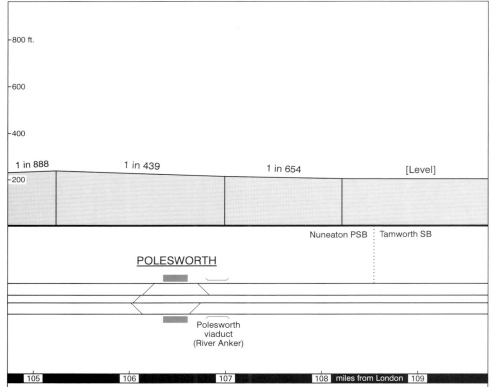

800 ft.

600

400

1 in 888   1 in 439   1 in 654   [Level]

200

Nuneaton PSB   Tamworth SB

POLESWORTH

Polesworth
viaduct
(River Anker)

105   106   107   108   miles from London   109

POLESWORTH : On the up fast line, a HST set passes through Polesworth station with 1A62, the 1338 Holyhead – Euston. The power cars are Nos. 43136, nearest the camera, and 43092. (HB 4/99)

38

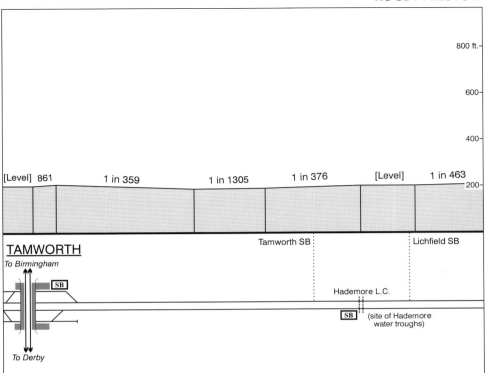

800 ft.-

600-

400-

[Level] 861   1 in 359   1 in 1305   1 in 376   [Level]   1 in 463

200-

Tamworth SB   Lichfield SB

TAMWORTH

To Birmingham

SB

Hademore L.C.

SB   (site of Hademore
water troughs)

To Derby

110   111   112   113   miles from London   114

TAMWORTH : This view of Tamworth station shows Class 86 No. 86259 Greater *MANCHESTER* ... propelling 1A53, the 1320 Preston – Euston. Note the steps leading from the low-level platform to Tamworth High level station on the Birmingham – Derby main line. (HB 4/99)

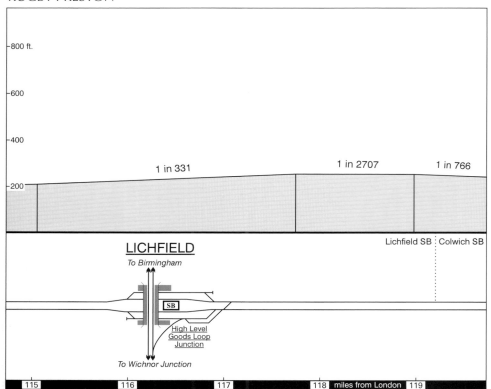

- 800 ft.
- 600
- 400
- 200

1 in 331   1 in 2707   1 in 766

Lichfield SB : Colwich SB

LICHFIELD

To Birmingham

SB

High Level
Goods Loop
Junction

To Wichnor Junction

115   116   117   118 miles from London 119

LICHFIELD : DVT No. 82138 heads 1M08, the 0615 Glasgow – Euston, southwards along the up fast line at Lichfield Trent Valley station. Of historical note is the LNWR 80 lever tumbler frame signalbox built in 1911 and situated between the up and down fast running lines. (HB 1/99)

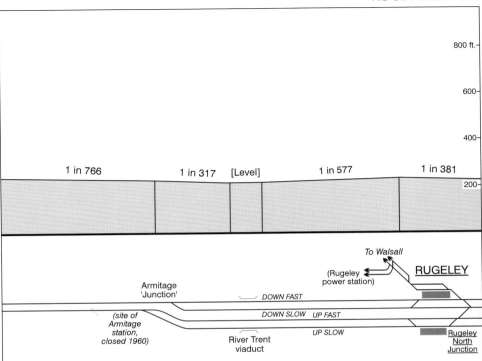

800 ft.–
600–
400–

1 in 766   1 in 317   [Level]   1 in 577   1 in 381

200–

To Walsall

(Rugeley
power station)   **RUGELEY**

Armitage
'Junction'   *DOWN FAST*

(site of
Armitage
station,
closed 1960)   *DOWN SLOW   UP FAST*

UP SLOW   Rugeley
North
Junction

River Trent
viaduct

120   121   122   123 miles from London 124

RUGELEY : Class 87 No. 87022 *Lew Adams The Black Prince* approaches Rugeley on 1H15, the 1600 Euston – Manchester. The lines to the right of the train lead to Cannock and Rugeley power station. (MB 9/99)

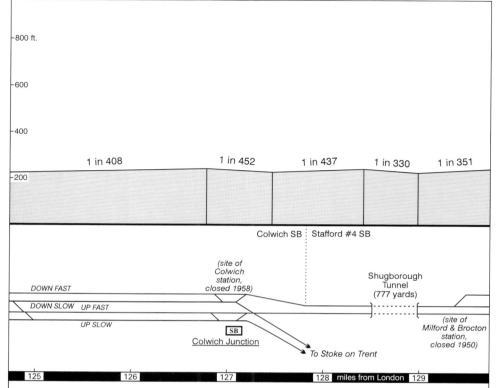

800 ft.

600

400

1 in 408   1 in 452   1 in 437   1 in 330   1 in 351

200

Colwich SB   Stafford #4 SB

(site of Colwich station, closed 1958)

Shugborough Tunnel (777 yards)

DOWN FAST

DOWN SLOW   UP FAST

UP SLOW

SB
Colwich Junction

To Stoke on Trent

(site of Milford & Brocton station, closed 1950)

125   126   127   128   miles from London   129

COLWICH : The majority of passenger services running between London and Manchester leave the WCML at Colwich. Due to a DVT failure, 1A32, the 0825 Manchester – Euston, formed of Mark 3 coaches, is seen passing Colwich signalbox behind an unidentified Class 86 locomotive. (MB 7/99)

42

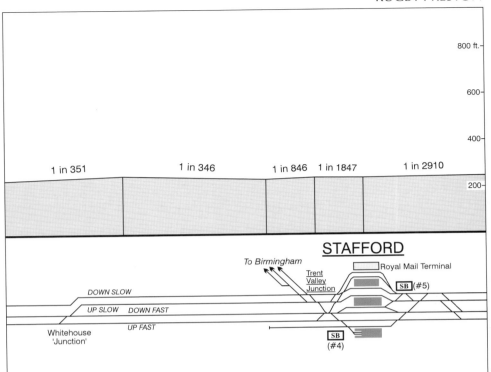

800 ft.—

600—

400—

1 in 351 1 in 346 1 in 846 1 in 1847 1 in 2910

200—

STAFFORD

To Birmingham

Trent Valley Junction

Royal Mail Terminal

DOWN SLOW

UP SLOW DOWN FAST

UP FAST

Whitehouse 'Junction'

SB (#5)

SB (#4)

130 131 132 133 miles from London 134

STAFFORD : The sweeping curve at Queensville, Stafford, is exaggerated in this view taken with a telephoto lens. Res Class 86 No. 86417 hauls a rake of 8 vans forming 1K00, Euston – Crewe postal. (HB 7/96)

43

STAFFORD : As the fog looms over Stafford station a Class 90, No. 90142 (above) hired from 'Freightliner', deputises for the booked Class 87 on 'Virgin Trains' service 1F12, the 0800 Euston - Liverpool Lime Street. The train awaits departure from platform 3 with the up and down fast lines visible between it and platform 1. (MB 9/99)

Having made the Stafford stop, Class 47 No. 47807 *The Lion of Vienna* (below) passes Stafford No. 5 signalbox with 1N41, the 0839 (Sunday) Birmingham - Preston. (HB 4/99)

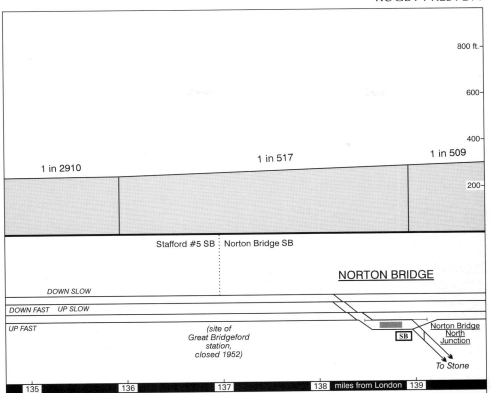

800 ft.

600

400

1 in 509

1 in 517

200

1 in 2910

Stafford #5 SB ⋮ Norton Bridge SB

NORTON BRIDGE

DOWN SLOW

DOWN FAST   UP SLOW

UP FAST

(site of
Great Bridgeford
station,
closed 1952)

SB

Norton Bridge
North
Junction

To Stone

135   136   137   138 miles from London 139

NORTON BRIDGE : In the background, the mainline to Stone, Stoke On Trent and Manchester leaves the WCML as Class 90 No. 90143 *Freightliner Coatbridge* passes Norton Bridge station on the up slow line with 4L97, Trafford Park - Felixstowe freightliner. (HB 8/98)

─800 ft.

─600

─400

| 1 in 509 | 1 in 650 | 1 in 590 |

─200

Norton Bridge SB : Madeley SB

DOWN SLOW   (Millmeece)

UP SLOW   *DOWN FAST*

UP FAST   *(site of
Standon Bridge
station,
closed 1952)*

140   **141**   **142**   **143** miles from London **144**

MILL MEECE : This popular photographic spot is located at grid reference 837327 on O/S Landranger map No. 127(Stafford & Telford). The shadows lengthen as a pair of Class 56s Nos. 56129+56072 (both sporting a 'Transrail' logo) proceed northward on 6S75, Sheerness – Mossend 'Enterprise'. (HB 8/98)

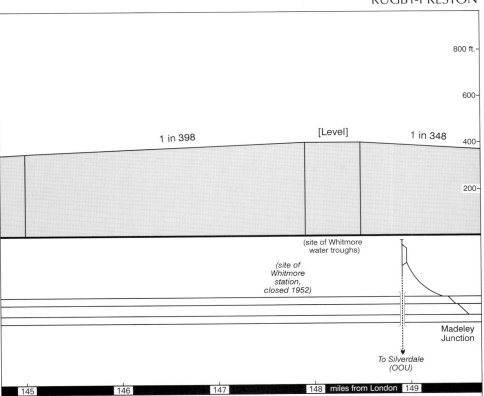

800 ft.

600

1 in 398   [Level]   1 in 348   400

200

(site of Whitmore
water troughs)

*(site of
Whitmore
station,
closed 1952)*

Madeley
Junction

*To Silverdale
(OOU)*

145   146   147   148   miles from London   149

WHITMORE : Passing the site of Whitmore station in mid-summer is Class 90 No. 90020 *Sir Michael Heron*, resplendent in EWS livery, heading 1S81, Plymouth – Glasgow mail. (HB 7/97)

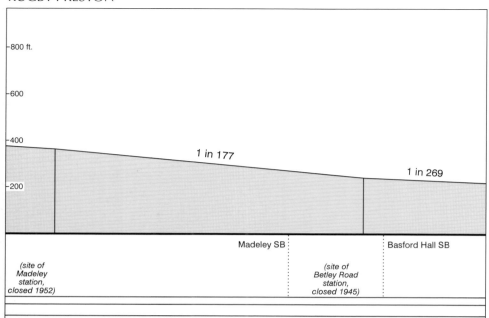

1 in 177

1 in 269

800 ft.

600

400

200

Madeley SB

Basford Hall SB

(site of
Madeley
station,
closed 1952)

(site of
Betley Road
station,
closed 1945)

SB
"Madeley"

SB
"Betley Road"

150   151   152   153   miles from London   154

MADELEY : The principal feature in this picture is the elevated signalbox at Madeley, junction for the 'mothballed' branch line to Silverdale Colliery (See map on previous page for details). A North Western Trains liveried EMU passes by with the 1419 Manchester Airport – Euston. (HB 4/99)

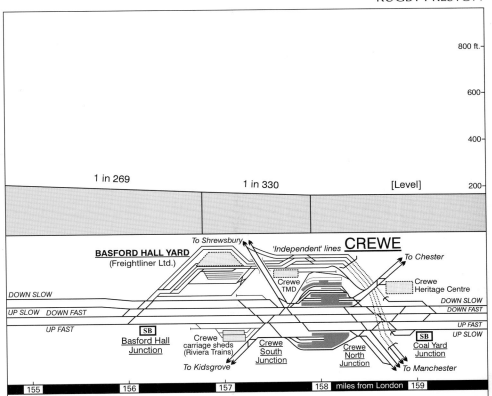

800 ft.-

600-

400-

1 in 269   1 in 330   [Level]   200-

To Shrewsbury   'Independent' lines   **CREWE**

BASFORD HALL YARD   To Chester
(Freightliner Ltd.)

Crewe   Crewe
TMD   Heritage Centre

DOWN SLOW   DOWN SLOW
                    DOWN FAST

UP SLOW   DOWN FAST

UP FAST   UP FAST
                    UP SLOW

SB   Crewe   SB
Basford Hall   carriage sheds   Crewe   Crewe   Coal Yard
Junction   (Riviera Trains)   South   North   Junction
                    Junction   Junction
To Kidsgrove   To Manchester

| 155 | 156 | 157 | 158 | miles from London | 159 |

CREWE BASFORD HALL : Class 47 No. 47302 leaves Basford Hall yard on a Trafford Park– Southampton freightliner and passes Basford Hall Junction signalbox; built in 1897 with a 70 lever tumbler frame. Most freightliner services convey two or three portions and are routed via Basford Hall yard, the most important hub on the freightliner network, where portions are swapped between trains. (AS 2/99)

CREWE : Looking south at a remodelled Crewe station, the up and down fast lines are adjacent to Class 47 No. 47217 (above) as it heads through platform 6 with a Barry Dock – Burn Naze train of 12 empty pressurised bogie tanks. These distinctive white tanks, with their orange warning band, are used to convey Vinyl Chloride Monomer and Liquefied Petroleum Gas. (AS 4/95)

Looking north, a wintry scene meets Class 87 No. 87011 *The Black Prince* (below) as it approaches with its DVT in tow on a late running Liverpool – Euston express. A class 37 can be seen in the background whilst the lines to Manchester deviate to the right. (BH 12/96)

CREWE 'INDEPENDENT' LINES : From Basford Hall, the 'Independent' lines take the majority of freight traffic away from the station area through tunnels to Coal Yard Junction and Sydney Bridge Junction, where the WCML and Manchester lines rejoin, respectively. A lightweight freight headed by Class 37 No. 37013 (above) is passed on the 'Independent' Lines by a train of steel coil from Ravenscraig, hauled by a pair of Class 87s. (BH)

At Coal yard Junction, Class 86 No. 86253 *The Manchester Guardian* (below) proceeds on a northbound express. Of note is the LMS 65 lever tumbler frame signal box built in 1939. (BH 5/97)

800 ft.

600

400

200

[Level]　　　　　　　　　　　1 in 411　　1 in 616　　1 in 2485

Crewe Coal Yard SB ┊ Winsford SB

DOWN SLOW
　　DOWN FAST
　　UP FAST
UP SLOW

*(site of
Minshull Vernon
Station,
closed 1942)*

160　　　161　　　162　　　163　miles from London　164

COPPENHALL : Class 47 No. 47231 proceeds south on the up slow line at Coppenhall Moss in charge of a relatively small freightliner train en-route from Garston to Felixstowe. On the down slow line Class 92 No. 92019 *Wagner* can be seen on signal trials. (BH 9/96)

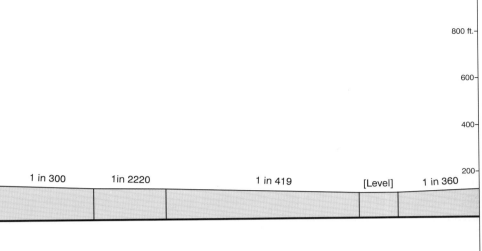

800 ft.-
600-
400-
200-

| 1 in 300 | 1in 2220 | 1 in 419 | [Level] | 1 in 360 |

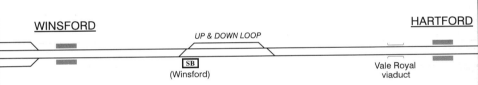

WINSFORD   HARTFORD

UP & DOWN LOOP

SB
(Winsford)

Vale Royal
viaduct

165   166   167   168   miles from London   169

WINSFORD : A dull afternoon at Winsford greets Class 92 No. 92006 *Louis Armand* at the helm of an even duller looking Crewe test train, heading south and a return to base. On 23 June 1999, the 0630 Euston – Glasgow, headed by 87027 *Wolf of Badenoch*, ran into two stationary Class 142 'Pacer' units where the running lines converge from 4 to 2 tracks. (MB 5/99)

53

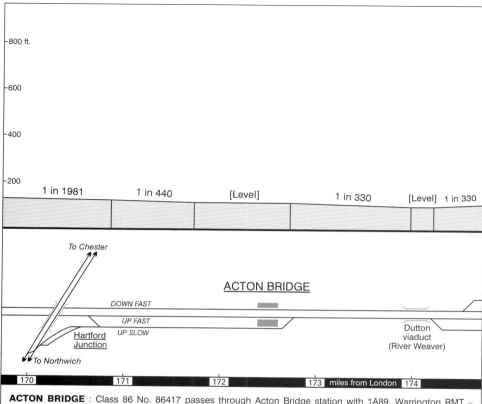

-800 ft.

-600

-400

-200

| 1 in 1981 | 1 in 440 | [Level] | 1 in 330 | [Level] | 1 in 330 |

To Chester

ACTON BRIDGE

DOWN FAST

UP FAST

UP SLOW

Hartford
Junction

To Northwich

Dutton
viaduct
(River Weaver)

170 171 172 173 miles from London 174

ACTON BRIDGE : Class 86 No. 86417 passes through Acton Bridge station with 1A89, Warrington RMT – Wilesden mail. The line behind the far right platform continues until Hartford Junction, where a spur leaves the WCML for Northwich. (MB 5/99)

54

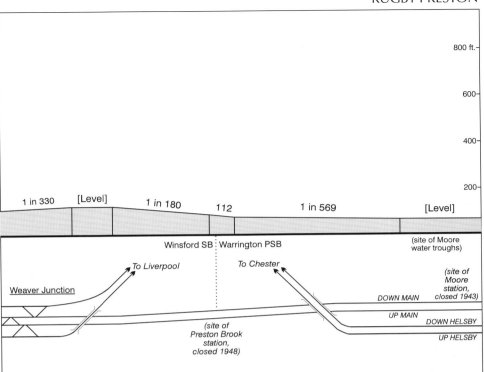

800 ft.–
600–
400–
200–

1 in 330 [Level] 1 in 180 112 1 in 569 [Level]

Winsford SB : Warrington PSB (site of Moore water troughs)

To Liverpool To Chester (site of Moore station, closed 1943)

Weaver Junction DOWN MAIN
UP MAIN
DOWN HELSBY
UP HELSBY

(site of Preston Brook station, closed 1948)

175 176 177 178 miles from London 179

MOORE : With the Warrington skyline dominating the background, Class 47 No. 47714 'drags' Class 90 No. 90023 on 5M83, Heaton – Crewe empty vans. Of note, top right, is the bridge spanning the Manchester Ship Canal at Acton Grange Junction. (BH 1/94)

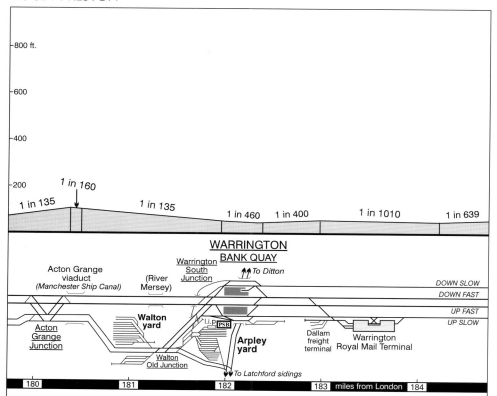

800 ft.

600

400

200

1 in 160

1 in 135

1 in 135

1 in 460   1 in 400   1 in 1010   1 in 639

WARRINGTON
BANK QUAY

Acton Grange
viaduct
(Manchester Ship Canal)

*(River
Mersey)*

Warrington
South
Junction

↑↑ *To Ditton*

DOWN SLOW

DOWN FAST

UP FAST

**Walton
yard**

l.i.p PSB

**Arpley
yard**

Dallam
freight
terminal

UP SLOW

Warrington
Royal Mail Terminal

Acton
Grange
Junction

Walton
Old Junction

↓↓ *To Latchford sidings*

| 180 | 181 | 182 | 183 | miles from London | 184 |

WARRINGTON BANK QUAY : The layout of Bank Quay station can be seen clearly in this view looking south of a Mark 3 DVT set approaching with a Carlisle – Euston service. Warrington power Signalbox is located just out of shot to the left of the Plasser unit. (AS 3/99)

WARRINGTON ARPLEY : The last Class 60 built, No. 60100 *Boar of Badenoch*, passes Arpley yard with an MGR coal train from Silverdale to Fiddlers Ferry power station. MGR services can only gain access to/from the power station by way of Latchford Sidings and the Low Level lines. (AS 2/97)

WARRINGTON LOW LEVEL : An EWS Class 60 No. 60012 emerges from underneath the WCML with loaded MGRs from Gladstone Dock to Fiddlers Ferry and passes another MGR heading in the opposite direction. The driver's signing-on point is adjacent to the semaphore signal. (AS 2/97)

WARRINGTON RAILNET : The RMT at Warrington is situated alongside the up side of the WCML between Warrington Bank Quay station and Winwick Junction. Class 47 No. 47737 *Resurgent* and Class 86 No. 86417 approach the terminal with empty stock. (AS 10/98)

WINWICK QUAY : A popular location with enthusiasts is the bridge spanning the WCML at Old Alder Lane, Winwick Quay. A Class 56, No. 56095, is seen approaching with 6E05, Stanlow – Humber empty LPG tanks. This train only traverses a short section of the WCML, between Acton Grange and Winwick junctions. (MR 8/99)

WINWICK JUNCTION : Rounding the curve from the south, Class 66 No. 66027 (above) approaches Winwick Junction with 6S72, Warington Arpley – Mossend 'Enterprise' service, comprised mainly of empty OTA timber wagons from Chirk and Shotton. (MR 7/99)

In the opposite direction, the lines from Earlstown trail in from the left and in the background is the famous English Electric Vulcan Foundry, now owned by Alstom. A pair of DRS Class 20s, Nos. 20302+20301 (below), pass with 7A73, Sellafield – Willesden nuclear train conveying flasks for Sizewell power station, Suffolk. (MR 7/99)

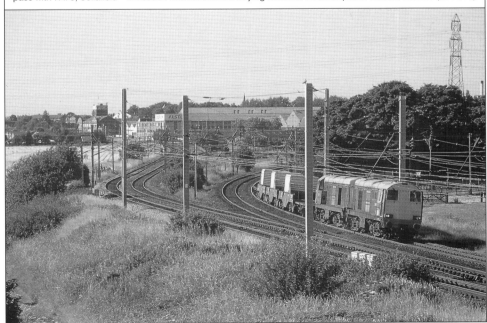

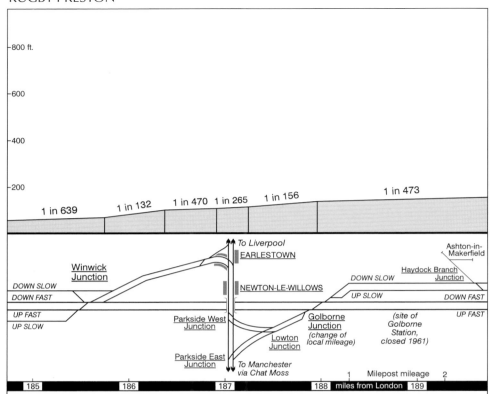

800 ft.

600

400

200

1 in 639   1 in 132   1 in 470   1 in 265   1 in 156   1 in 473

To Liverpool

EARLESTOWN

Ashton-in-Makerfield

Winwick Junction

NEWTON-LE-WILLOWS

Haydock Branch Junction

DOWN SLOW

DOWN SLOW

DOWN FAST

DOWN FAST

UP SLOW

DOWN FAST

UP FAST

Golborne Junction

(site of Golborne Station, closed 1961)

UP FAST

UP SLOW

Parkside West Junction

Lowton Junction

(change of local mileage)

UP SLOW

Parkside East Junction

To Manchester via Chat Moss

Milepost mileage

185   186   187   188   miles from London   189

RED BANK : Located between Winwick and Golborne Junctions, Class 90 No. 90146 heads past Red Bank, with 6M64, Elgin – Dee Marsh train of timber. The following day traction for this train was switched to a Class 56. (BH 3/96)

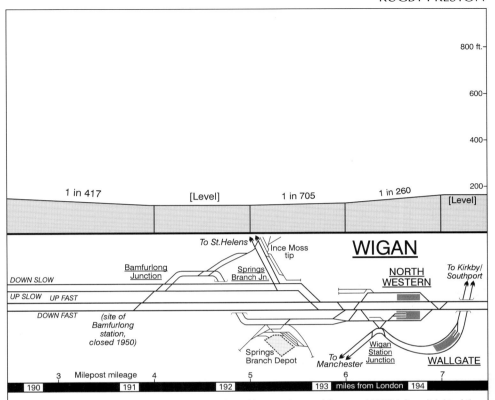

800 ft.-

600-

400-

200-

1 in 417

[Level]

1 in 705

1 in 260

[Level]

To St.Helens

Ince Moss
tip

WIGAN

Bamfurlong
Junction

Springs
Branch Jn.

NORTH
WESTERN

To Kirkby/
Southport

DOWN SLOW

UP SLOW   UP FAST

DOWN FAST   (site of
Bamfurlong
station,
closed 1950)

Springs
Branch Depot

To
Manchester

Wigan
Station
Junction

WALLGATE

3   Milepost mileage   4   5   6   7

190   191   192   193 miles from London 194

WIGAN SPRINGS BRANCH : This view shows Ince Moss engineers sidings and TMD, left and right of the WCML, respectively. On the TMD can be seen locomotive classes 08, 20, 31, 47 and 60 stabled although, at the time of writing, Springs Branch was closed and used only to stable withdrawn locomotives. The Class 47 in shot is No. 47314 *Transmark* heading south with chemical tanks. (AS 5/95)

WIGAN : Class 66, No. 66099, heads 6V23, Hardendale – Margam lime train through Wigan North Western station where, partly obscured by the train, can be seen the hexagonal waiting room on the up platform, known locally as the "Gazebo". (MR 7/99)

STANDISH : Track rationalisation carried out under the 1970s upgrade of the WCML is clearly evident in this view of Class 60 No. 60056 *William Beveridge* near Standish with 6M19, Jarrow – Stanlow oil train. (BH 5/95)

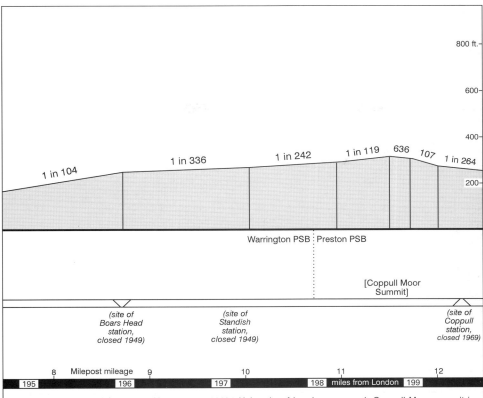

800 ft.─

600─

400─

1 in 104   1 in 336   1 in 242   1 in 119   636   107   1 in 264

200─

Warrington PSB ┊ Preston PSB

[Coppull Moor
Summit]

(site of
Boars Head
station,
closed 1949)

(site of
Standish
station,
closed 1949)

(site of
Coppull
station,
closed 1969)

| 8 | Milepost mileage | 9 | | 10 | | 11 | miles from London | 12 |

195   196   197   198   199

COPPULL : A pair of Class 86s, Nos. 86605+86634 *University of London*, approach Coppull Moor summit in charge of 4S87, Felixstowe – Coatbridge freightliner; Local milepost 11¼ is adjacent to the locomotives. (MR 7/99)

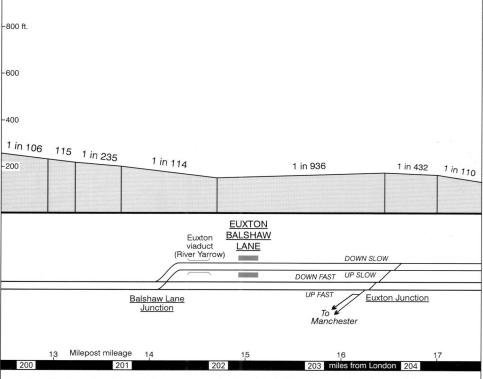

-800 ft.

-600

-400

-200

1 in 106   115   1 in 235   1 in 114   1 in 936   1 in 432   1 in 110

EUXTON
BALSHAW
LANE

Euxton
viaduct
(River Yarrow)

DOWN SLOW

DOWN FAST   UP SLOW

Balshaw Lane
Junction

UP FAST   Euxton Junction

To
Manchester

13   Milepost mileage   14   15   16   17

200   201   202   203   miles from London   204

BALSHAW LANE : The latest station to open on the WCML is Balshaw Lane, although no mainline expresses call there. The platforms are situated adjacent to the up and down slow lines, where a Class 150 unit, No. 150141, leaves with a Morecambe – Liverpool service. (AS 10/98)

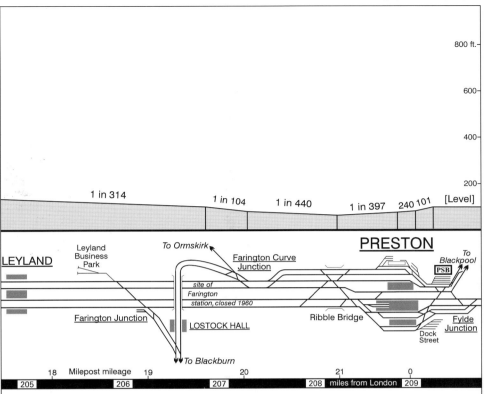

800 ft.–

600–

400–

200–

[Level]

1 in 314

1 in 104

1 in 440

1 in 397

240 101

LEYLAND

Leyland
Business
Park

To Ormskirk

Farington Curve
Junction

PRESTON

To
Blackpool

PSB

site of
Farington
station, closed 1960

Farington Junction

LOSTOCK HALL

Ribble Bridge

Fylde
Junction

Dock
Street

To Blackburn

18   Milepost mileage   19   20   21   0

205   206   207   208 miles from London 209

LEYLAND : Looking north, a spartan looking Leyland station plays host to Class 150 and Class 142 units as they call with services to Liverpool and Manchester respectively. (AS 3/95)

PRESTON : The restored main entrance to Preston station looms high above the platform canopy, as Class 86 No. 86231 *Starlight Express* (above), deputising for the booked Class 87, waits departure time with 1S86, the 1635 Euston – Glasgow. (MR 7/99)

At 1910 hrs, the sun casts long shadows onto platform 2 at Preston station, where a Class 158 unit waits time on the 'Northern Spirit' 1847 Blackpool – York. Meanwhile, mail unit No. 325006 *John Grierson* (below) hurries through platform 3 with 1S96, Willesden – Shieldmuir Railnet service; (MR 7/99)

**Preston
to
Carlisle**

PRESTON-CARLISLE

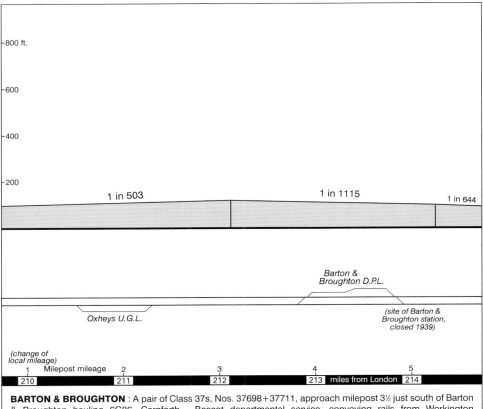

- 800 ft.
- 600
- 400
- 200

1 in 503 — 1 in 1115 — 1 in 644

Barton &
Broughton D.P.L.

Oxheys U.G.L.

(site of Barton &
Broughton station,
closed 1939)

(change of
local mileage)

Milepost mileage — miles from London

1	2	3	4	5
210	211	212	213	214

BARTON & BROUGHTON : A pair of Class 37s, Nos. 37698+37711, approach milepost 3½ just south of Barton & Broughton hauling 6G86, Carnforth - Bescot departmental service, conveying rails from Workington steelworks. The leading class 37 carries the black & orange 'Loadhaul' livery. (MR 7/99)

68

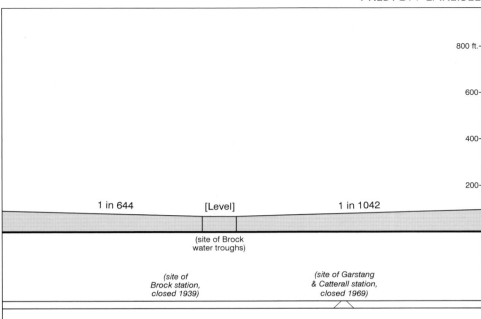

800 ft.–

600–

400–

200–

1 in 644   [Level]   1 in 1042

(site of Brock
water troughs)

(site of
Brock station,
closed 1939)

(site of Garstang
& Catterall station,
closed 1969)

6   Milepost mileage   7   8   9   10
215   216   217   218 miles from London 219

BROCK : A solitary Class 153 unit No.153367 approaches the foot crossing at Brock with a Morecambe - Liverpool service; two bridges spanning the M6 motorway can be seen to the far right of the picture. (AS 6/96)

-800 ft.

-600

-400

-200

[Level]	1 in 1199	[Level]

(site of Scorton station, closed 1939)

(site of Bay Horse station, closed 1960)

'Six Arches' viaduct (River Wyre)

11	Milepost mileage	12		13		14		15
210		211		212		213	miles from London	214

HOLLINS LANE : The gentle meandering curves on this stretch of the WCML near Hollins Lane give an almost branch line feel to this view of Class 31 No. 31200, sporting Coal Sector decals, ambling north with 7C40, Valley - Sellafield British Nuclear Fuels train. (BH 4/92)

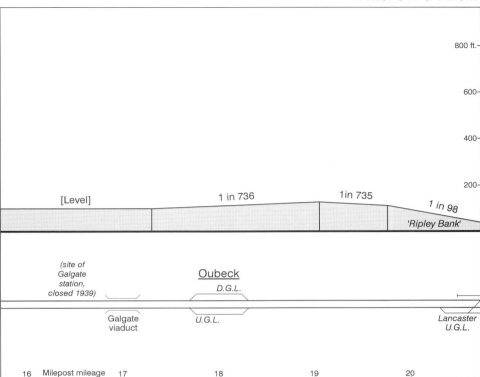

800 ft.-

600-

400-

200-

[Level]   1 in 736   1in 735   *1 in 98*

'Ripley Bank'

(site of Galgate station, closed 1939)

Oubeck

D.G.L.

Galgate viaduct   *U.G.L.*   Lancaster *U.G.L.*

16   Milepost mileage   17   18   19   20

225   226   227   228   miles from London   229

OUBECK : An unidentified Class 86 is seen just south of Oubeck loops with 1V04, Shieldmuir - Bristol mail vans; the down loop can just be made out to the left of the last mail van. (MR 7/99)

71

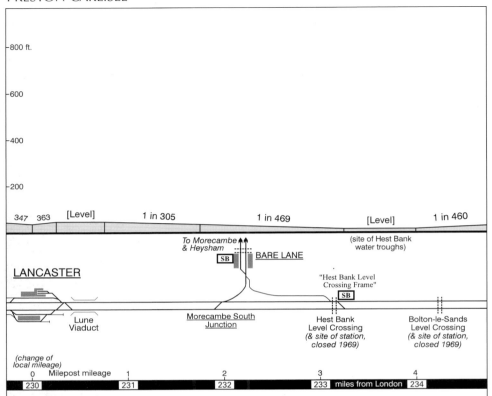

800 ft.

600

400

200

| 347 | 363 | [Level] | 1 in 305 | 1 in 469 | [Level] | 1 in 460 |

To Morecambe & Heysham

(site of Hest Bank water troughs)

SB **BARE LANE**

LANCASTER

"Hest Bank Level Crossing Frame"

SB

Lune Viaduct

Morecambe South Junction

Hest Bank Level Crossing *(& site of station, closed 1969)*

Bolton-le-Sands Level Crossing *(& site of station, closed 1969)*

(change of local mileage)

| 0 | Milepost mileage | 1 | | 2 | | 3 | miles from London | 4 |

230 | 231 | 232 | 233 | 234

LANCASTER : A splendid contrast of light and shade greets the eye in this composition of Class 92, No. 92019 *Wagner*, sweeping through the fast lines at Lancaster station with 4M74, Mossend Euroterminal - Wembley 'Intermodal'. Of special interest is the old, but distinctive, wrought iron & glass panelled footbridge linking the main up and down platforms. (MR 7/99)

HEST BANK : Class 92 No. 92006 *Louis Armand* (above) heads 4S90, Willesden Euroterminal - Mossend 'Intermodal' past Hest Bank, the only point where the WCML actually runs next to the coast, which can be seen at the top right of the picture. (MR 08/99)

Passing the signalbox and level crossing at Hest Bank is Class 60 No. 60093 *Jack Stirk* (below) hauling 6V41, the Irvine - Burngullow 'Silver Bullet' (slightly drab looking) empty china clay tanks. (MR /98)

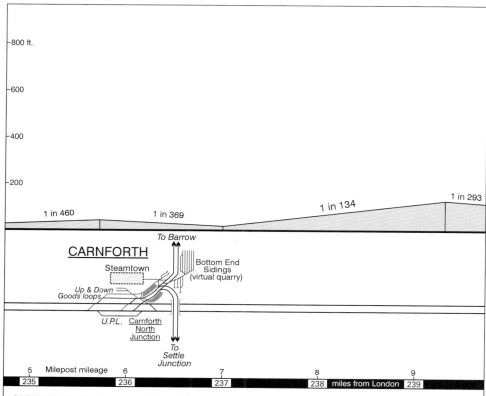

800 ft.

600

400

200

1 in 293

1 in 134

1 in 460

1 in 369

To Barrow

CARNFORTH

Steamtown

Bottom End
Sidings
(virtual quarry)

Up & Down
Goods loops

U.P.L.   Carnforth
North
Junction

To
Settle
Junction

5	Milepost mileage	6		7		8		9
235		236		237		238	miles from London	239

CARNFORTH : The view towards Carnforth shows the up and down loops to the south of the station as a Class 142 unit No. 142075 forms a cross country service from Leeds to Lancaster. The train traversed the 'Little North Western' route before joining the WCML at Carnforth. (AS 3/96)

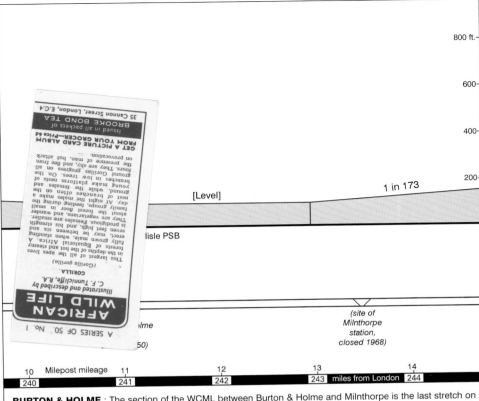

800 ft.
600
400
200

[Level]   1 in 173

lisle PSB

(site of
Milnthorpe
station,
closed 1968)

lme

50)

| 10 | Milepost mileage | 11 | | 12 | | 13 | | 14 |
| 240 | | 241 | | 242 | | 243 | miles from London | 244 |

BURTON & HOLME : The section of the WCML between Burton & Holme and Milnthorpe is the last stretch on the level before the climb to Grayrigg and Shap. Class 90 No. 90127 *Allerton T&RS Depot* passes Holme with 4M74, 'Intermodal' service from Mossend to Wembley. (AS 6/97)

75

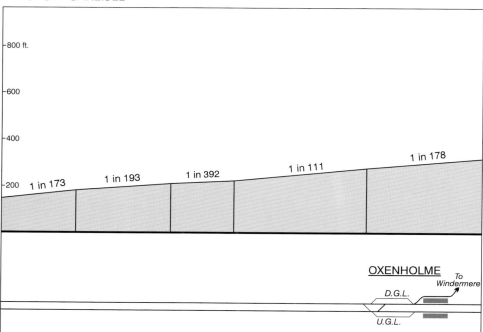

800 ft.

600

400

1 in 178

1 in 111

200 1 in 173   1 in 193   1 in 392

OXENHOLME
To Windermere

D.G.L.

U.G.L.

| 15 | Milepost mileage | 16 | | 17 | | 18 | miles from London | 19 |
| 245 | | 246 | | 247 | | 248 | | 249 |

OXENHOLME : The winter sunshine greets the first service of the day at Oxenholme station. DVT No. 82121 *Carlisle Cathedral* leads 1M64, the 1230 Glasgow - Euston, which was delayed due to the overrun of engineering work, past the corrugated metal canopy spanning the down platform and Windermere branch. (DM 1/99)

"Grayrigg Bank"

1 in 106

1 in 131

800 ft.-

600-

400-

200-

1 in 104   213   1 in 124

Docker
viaduct

20   Milepost mileage   21   22   23   miles from London   24
250   251   252   253   254

DOCKER : Locomotive double-heading on freightliner services over the northern banks is still a common sight; as seen here at Docker, where a pair of Class 86/6s Nos. 86635+86621 head south with 4O32, Coatbridge - Southampton freightliner. (PJR 7/97)

77

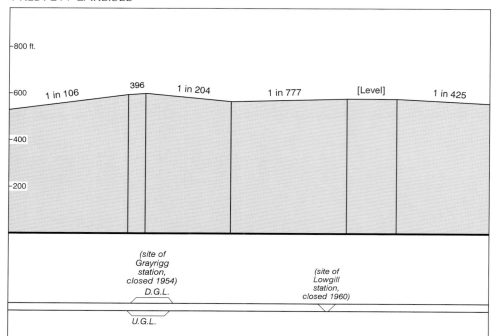

-800 ft.

-600   1 in 106   396   1 in 204   1 in 777   [Level]   1 in 425

-400

-200

*(site of
Grayrigg
station,
closed 1954)*
D.G.L.

*(site of
Lowgill
station,
closed 1960)*

U.G.L.

25   Milepost mileage   26   27   28   29
255   256   257   258 miles from London 259

GRAYRIGG : A Class 60, No. 60097 *Pillar*, begins the descent from Grayrigg with an MGR train of opencast coal; 7F60 Carlisle London Road - Fiddlers Ferry. Traces of snow still remain on the fells in the background as Winter gradually peters out. (PJR 2/96)

LOW GILL : The B6257 road follows the route of the closed Low Gill to Ingleton branch down the Lune valley and is crossed by an unidentified Class 86 (above) heading 5MO6, Polmadie - Crewe South yard empty mail vans. The hamlet of Beck Foot is behind the photographer. (DM 5/97)

In the background, the M6 motorway can be glimpsed as Class 37 No. 37504 (below) sweeps into the cutting at Low Gill with 6S42, Llanwern - Mossend steel empties. (BH 4/92)

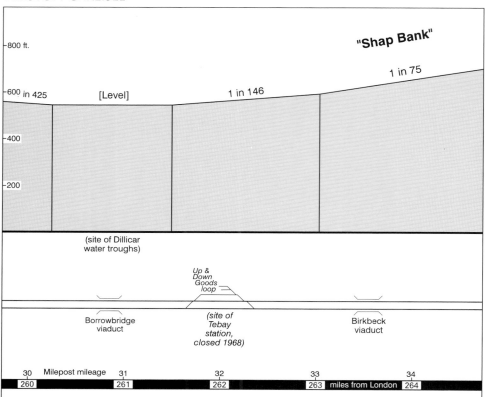

"Shap Bank"

-800 ft.

-600 in 425   [Level]   1 in 146   1 in 75

-400

-200

(site of Dillicar
water troughs)

Up &
Down
Goods
loop

Borrowbridge
viaduct

(site of
Tebay
station,
closed 1968)

Birkbeck
viaduct

30   Milepost mileage   31   32   33   34
260   261   262   263 miles from London 264

TEBAY : The railway cottages at Tebay stand out on the hillside as an HST (power cars 43088/43098) passes by with 1S71, the 0720 Penzance - Edinburgh "Cornish Scot". The 5.5 miles from Tebay to Shap summit posed such a bottleneck to steam that signalling was divided into 4 block sections. (BH 8/95)

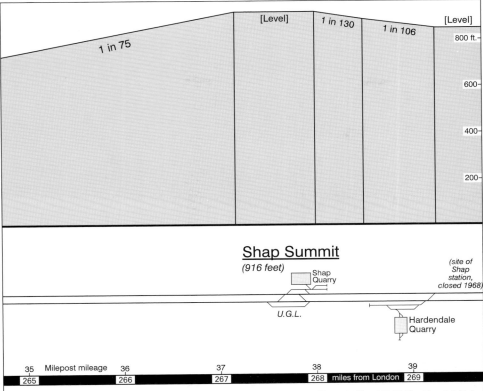

	[Level]	1 in 130	1 in 106	[Level]
1 in 75				800 ft.–

Shap Summit
(916 feet)

Shap Quarry

(site of Shap station, closed 1968)

U.G.L.

Hardendale Quarry

35	Milepost mileage	36		37		38		39	
265		266		267		268	miles from London	269	

SHAP SUMMIT : Shap summit lies in a cutting 916ft. above sea level. Class 86 No. 86244 *The Royal British Legion* heads the 1230 Glasgow - Coventry at the summit and overtakes Class 31 No. 31203 in the up loop on a train of continuous welded rails. (DM 10/95)

81

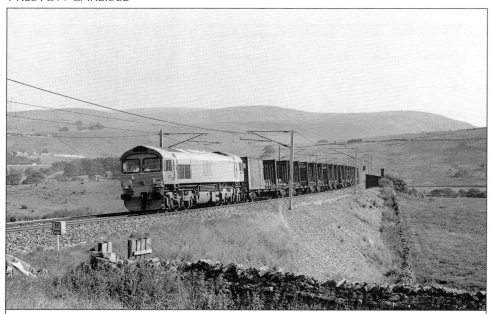

GREENHOLME : The northern stretches of the WCML provide the ideal territory for new locomotives and rolling stock to be put through their paces and two such examples are recorded here. Class 59 No. 59104 (above) tackles the climb to Shap summit at Greenholme with the return 4Z69 Carnforth - Mossend, which incorporated brake tests on both Shap and Beattock gradients. (BH 7/91)

Class 92 No. 92032 *Cesar Franck* (below) is seen at the same location on a test run involving the 'Eurostar' night stock which, unfortunately, have been placed in store at MoD sidings around the country and will not see the 'light of day' on active revenue earning service! (MB 4/97)

HARDENDALE : British Steel's quarry at Hardendale provides regular rail-borne flows of lime to Port Talbot and Lackenby steelworks. Class 66 No. 66099 prepares to leave the quarry and join the WCML with 6V23, Hardendale - Margam lime train. Note the Lime kilns and redundant overhead catenary masts. (MB 7/99)

HARRISONS SIDINGS : A pair of Class 86s Nos. 86633 *Wulfruna* and 86607 *The Institution of Electrical Engineers* pass Harrisons Sidings with 4L60, Coatbridge - Felixstowe freightliner. A quarry is located here providing road borne aggregate. (PJR 7/97)

PRESTON-CARLISLE

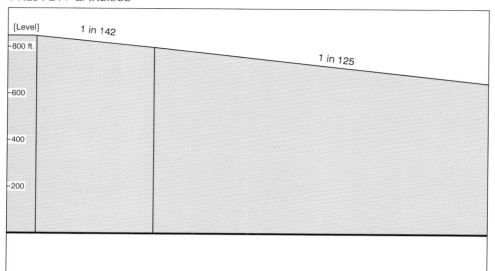

[Level]

1 in 142

800 ft.

1 in 125

-600

-400

-200

Harrisons
D.G.L.

Harrisons
quarry

40	Milepost mileage	41		42		43	miles from London	44
270		271		272		273		274

THRIMBY : On the southbound, more gentler, climb to Shap a Class 90, No. 90018, is seen passing the infant River Leith near Thrimby with 5M06, Polmadie - Crewe empty mail vans. (DM 7/97)

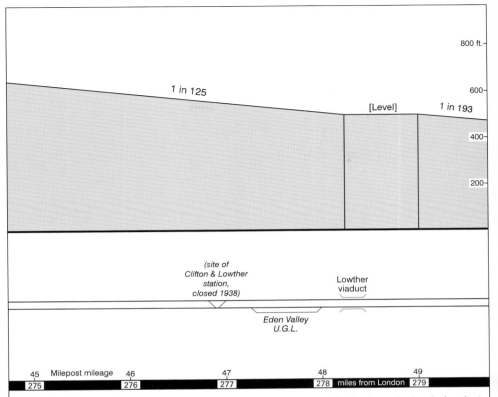

800 ft.-

1 in 125

600-

[Level]   1 in 193

400-

200-

(site of
Clifton & Lowther
station,
closed 1938)

Lowther
viaduct

Eden Valley
U.G.L.

45   Milepost mileage   46   47   48   49
275   276   277   278 miles from London 279

REDHILLS : A beautifully lit composition sees Class 47 No. 47219 *Arnold Kunzler* at the head of a short southbound MoD freight at Redhills, near Penrith. The down goods line is in the foreground, close to where the WCML crosses the River Eamont (see map on next page for details). (DM 1/97)

800 ft.

600

193   1 in 191   1 in 616   [Level]   1 in 539   1 in 186

400

200

PENRITH

DOWN GOODS

Eamont
Viaduct

50   Milepost mileage   51   52   53   54
280   281   282   283   miles from London   284

PENRITH : The track layout at Penrith is well illustrated in this view of Class 86 No. 86206 *City of Stoke on Trent* making the station stop with 1S48, the 0905 Birmingham New Street - Edinburgh. The down goods line and former goods yard are featured to the right of the picture. (MB 7/99)

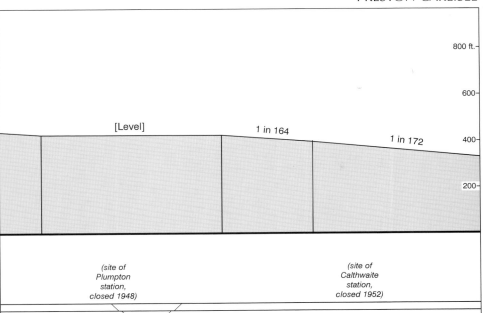

800 ft.

600

[Level]   1 in 164

                                      1 in 172   400

200

(site of
Plumpton
station,
closed 1948)

(site of
Calthwaite
station,
closed 1952)

Plumpton U.G.L.

| 55 | Milepost mileage | 56 | | 57 | | 58 | | 59 |
| 285 | | 286 | | 287 | | 288 | miles from London | 289 |

PLUMPTON : The longest level stretch of the WCML between Oxenholme and Carlisle (just 2 miles) lies close to Plumpton; mixed liveries prevail as Class 86 No. 86209 *City of Coventry* heads past the hamlet with 1M33, the 1440 Edinburgh - Birmingham. (DM 5/98)

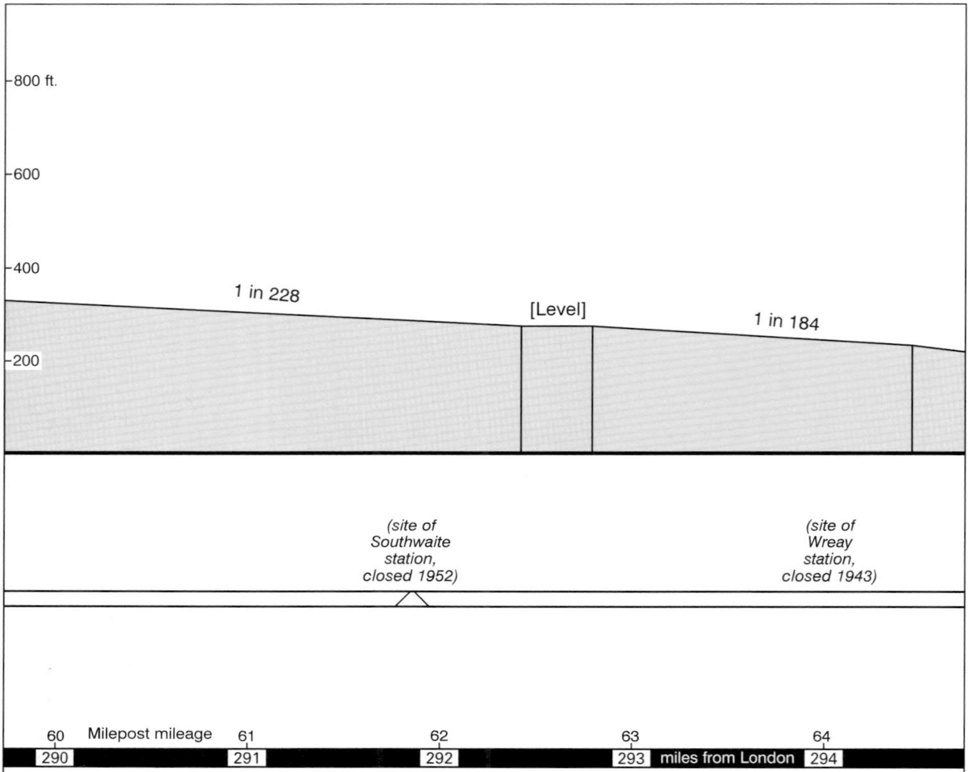

800 ft.

600

400

1 in 228

[Level]

1 in 184

200

(site of
Southwaite
station,
closed 1952)

(site of
Wreay
station,
closed 1943)

| 60 | Milepost mileage | 61 | | 62 | | 63 | | 64 |
| 290 | | 291 | | 292 | | 293 | miles from London | 294 |

SOUTHWAITE : An idyllic rural landscape greets the eye in this composition of Transrail Class 60 No. 60061 *Alexander Graham Bell*, heading south with 6M46, Redcar - Hardendale empty lime hoppers. (DM 6/98)

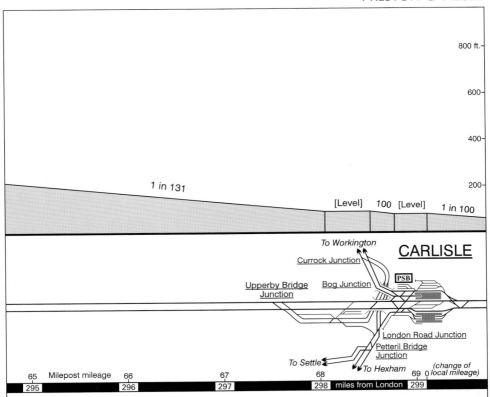

1 in 131

[Level] 100 [Level] 1 in 100

800 ft.
600
400
200

To Workington

Currock Junction

CARLISLE

PSB

Upperby Bridge Junction

Bog Junction

London Road Junction

Petteril Bridge Junction

To Settle

To Hexham

(change of local mileage)

| 65 | Milepost mileage | 66 | | 67 | | 68 | miles from London | 69 | 0 |
| 295 | | 296 | | 297 | | 298 | | 299 | |

CARLISLE : *Contre jour* - Class 86 No. 86258 *Talyllyn The First Preserved Railway* makes its way into Citadel station with 1S46, the 0655 Birmingham - Glasgow. To the right of the Class 86 the Cumbrian Coast line peels away, while further right a snowplough, 08s and a Class 153 unit share Wapping sidings. On the left, the London Road lines drop steeply away, giving access to the Newcastle and Settle routes. (DM 1/99)

CARLISLE CITADEL : A pair of Class 86s, Nos. 86627 & 86613 (above), sporting the latest 'Freightliner' branding, pass through the station with 4L60, Coatbridge - Felixstowe freightliner. Note the screenwall and the bay platforms, used by local Tyne valley passenger services. (MB 8/99)

The northern end of Citadel station plays host to Class 90 No. 90002 *Mission Impossible* (below), propelling "The Royal Scot" (1M25, 1150 Glasgow - Euston), whilst BSC liveried Class 60 No. 60033 *Tees Steel Express* rumbles through platform 3 with MGR empties. (DM 1/99)

**Carlisle
to
Glasgow**

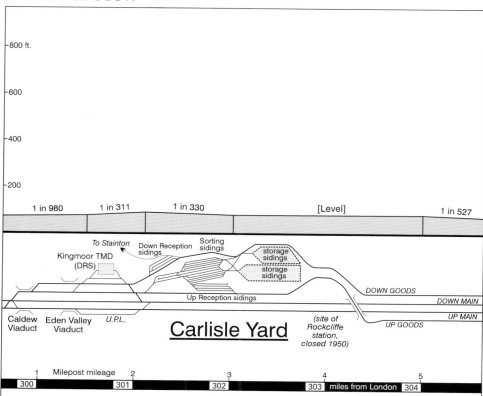

800 ft.

600

400

200

| 1 in 980 | 1 in 311 | 1 in 330 | [Level] | 1 in 527 |

To Stainton

Down Reception sidings

Sorting sidings

storage sidings

storage sidings

Kingmoor TMD (DRS)

Up Reception sidings

DOWN GOODS

DOWN MAIN

Caldew Viaduct   Eden Valley Viaduct   U.P.L.

Carlisle Yard

(site of Rockcliffe station, closed 1950)

UP MAIN

UP GOODS

1   Milepost mileage   2   3   4   5

| 300 | 301 | 302 | 303 | miles from London | 304 |

CARLISLE KINGMOOR : Storm clouds gather on a freezing Saturday afternoon and the last rays of sunshine fall on Class 56 No. 56072 as it leaves Kingmoor yard with an up MGR. The sad decline of Kingmoor as a marshalling yard can be seen by the amount of track that has been lifted. (DM 1/99)

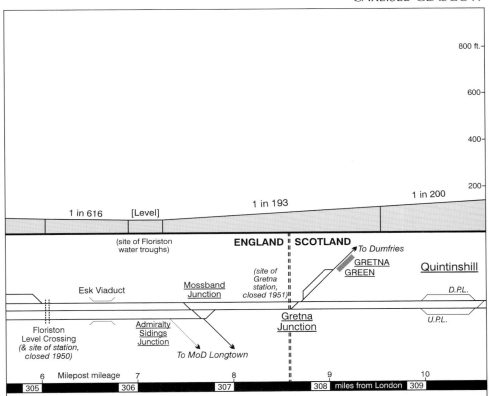

800 ft.-

600-

400-

200-

1 in 200

1 in 193

1 in 616   [Level]

(site of Floriston
water troughs)

ENGLAND ⫶ SCOTLAND

To Dumfries

(site of
Gretna
station,
closed 1951)⫶

GRETNA
GREEN

Quintinshill

Esk Viaduct

Mossband
Junction

D.P.L.

Gretna
Junction

U.P.L.

Floriston
Level Crossing
(& site of station,
closed 1950)

Admiralty
Sidings
Junction

To MoD Longtown

6   Milepost mileage   7   8   9   10

305   306   307   308   miles from London   309

ESK VIADUCT : Photographed from the Metal Bridge Inn on the bank of the River Esk, an unidentified Class 90 heads 4O27, Coatbridge - Southampton freightliner, across the viaduct spanning the river, which ultimately flows into the Solway Firth . (MB 7/99)

93

GRETNA : Class 47 No. 47791 passes Gretna Junction sporting "The Great Briton" headboard as it heads this luxury charter into Scotland. The former GSWR lines to Dumfries can be seen trailing away to the right of the train. (PJR 9/96)

QUINTINSHILL : A Class 86, No. 86256 *Pebble Mill*, hauling 1S49, the 1031 Birmingham International - Edinburgh, passes the site of Britain's worst rail disaster. On May 22nd 1915, a troop train collided with a Scotch express at Quintinshill resulting in an estimated 200+ servicemen losing their lives. (PJR 1/99)

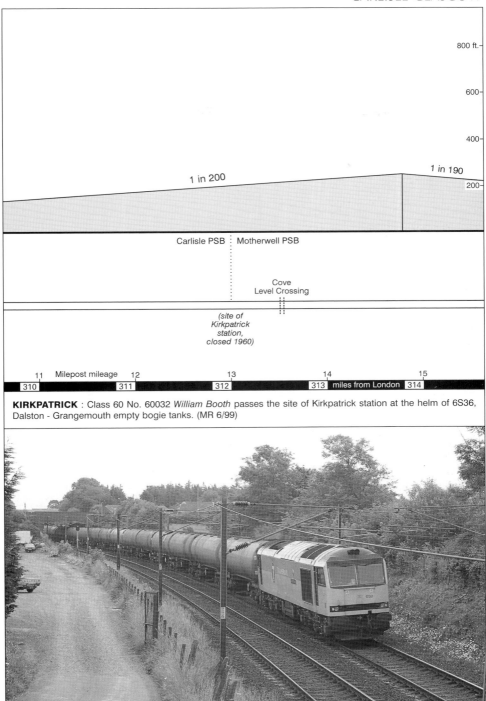

800 ft.-

600-

400-

1 in 190

1 in 200

200-

Carlisle PSB | Motherwell PSB

Cove
Level Crossing

*(site of
Kirkpatrick
station,
closed 1960)*

11   Milepost mileage   12   13   14   15
310   311   312   313   miles from London   314

KIRKPATRICK : Class 60 No. 60032 *William Booth* passes the site of Kirkpatrick station at the helm of 6S36, Dalston - Grangemouth empty bogie tanks. (MR 6/99)

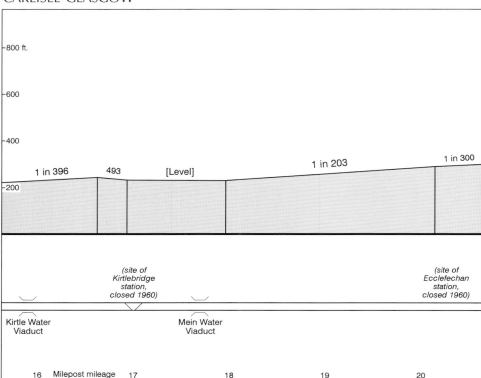

800 ft.

600

400

1 in 396   493   [Level]   1 in 203   1 in 300

200

*(site of
Kirtlebridge
station,
closed 1960)*

*(site of
Ecclefechan
station,
closed 1960)*

Kirtle Water
Viaduct

Mein Water
Viaduct

16   Milepost mileage   17   18   19   20

315   316   317   318   miles from London   319

KIRTLEBRIDGE : As sheep graze in a field below, Class 86 No. 86236 *Josiah Wedgewood* is seen heading 1V50, the 0840 Glasgow - Penzance across Mein Water viaduct. (MB 5/99)

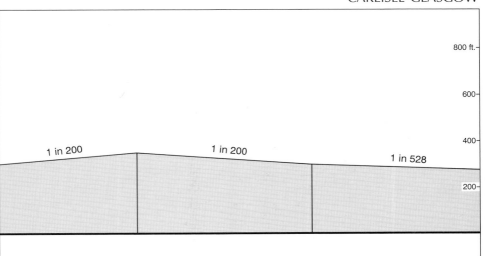

800 ft.

600

400

1 in 200

1 in 200

1 in 528

200

*Lockerbie
D.P.L.*

Milk Water
Viaduct

*Lockerbie
U.P.L.*

21   Milepost mileage   22   23   24   25
320   321   322   323   miles from London   324

CASTLEMILK : Class 90 No. 90023 sweeps round the curve at Castlemilk with 6M79, Mossend - Bescot 'Connectrail', formed mainly of Cargowagons. (PJR 9/94)

-800 ft.

-600

-400

1 in 528   [Level]   1 in 880

-200

LOCKERBIE

(site of Nethercleugh station, closed 1960)

U.P.L.

Dryfe Water
Viaduct

26   Milepost mileage   27   28   29   30

325   326   327   328   miles from London   329

LOCKERBIE : The unique 'Piggyback' wagons entered service in June 1998, with Parcelforce being the first customer. Their trailers are seen passing through Lockerbie on 4S99, Willesden - Mossend 'Intermodal' service, with Class 86 No. 86424 at the helm. (MB 7/99)

800 ft.-

600-

400-

1 in 366   1 in 326   1 in 330   [Level]

200-

(site of
Dinwoodie
station,
closed 1960)

(site of
Wamphray
station,
closed 1960)

31   Milepost mileage   32   33   34   35
330   331   332   333 miles from London 334

ANNANDALE : After Lockerbie the WCML passes through pastoral Annandale until Beattock, where the real climb begins in earnest. A pair of DRS Class 20s, Nos. 20302+20304, amble southwards near the hamlets of Murthat with 7M50, Torness - Carlisle Kingmoor nuclear flasks. (MB 7/99)

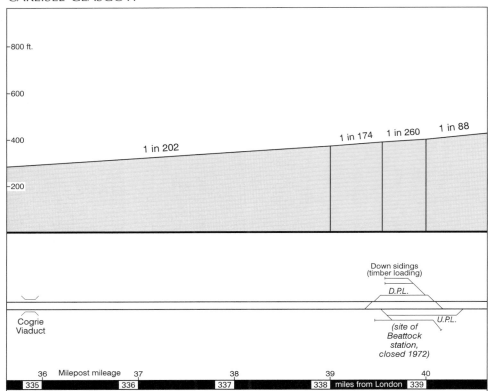

800 ft.

600

400

1 in 202

1 in 174   1 in 260   1 in 88

200

Down sidings
(timber loading)

D.P.L.

Cogrie
Viaduct

U.P.L.

(site of
Beattock
station,
closed 1972)

36   Milepost mileage   37

38

39

40

335   336   337   338   miles from London   339

BEATTOCK : The passing loops at Beattock are visible in this shot of Class 86 No. 86250 *The Glasgow Herald* on the 1420 Euston - Glasgow at the start of the 10 mile climb to Beattock summit. At the time, all Euston - Glasgow services were diagrammed for Class 87s - the "Electric Scots". (PJR 9/90)

100

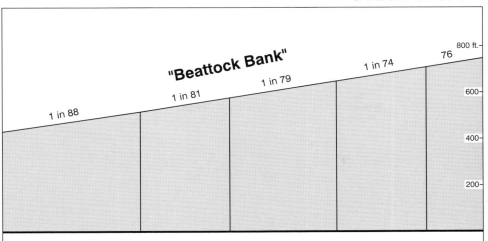

"Beattock Bank"

1 in 88   1 in 81   1 in 79   1 in 74   76

800 ft.-
600-
400-
200-

41   Milepost mileage   42   43   44   45
340   341   342   343 miles from London 344

GRESKINE : This photograph of Greskine illustrates the extent to which the new A74(M) motorway (far right) has disfigured the landscape in the vicinity of Beattock; Class 325 units Nos. 325012 & 325006 head south with 1M90, Shieldmuir RMT - London mail. (MB 5/99)

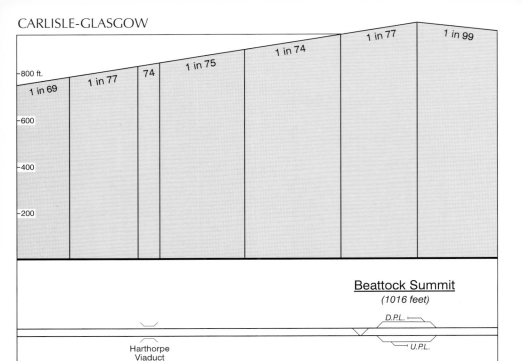

1 in 77
1 in 99
800 ft.
74
1 in 75
1 in 74
1 in 69
1 in 77
600
400
200

Beattock Summit
(1016 feet)

D.P.L.

U.P.L.

Harthorpe
Viaduct

46   Milepost mileage   47   48   49   50

| 345 | | 346 | | 347 | | 348 | miles from London | 349 |

BEATTOCK SUMMIT : At 1,016 ft., Beattock summit represents the highest point the WCML reaches above sea level. Running to time, Class 92 No. 92012 *Thomas Hardy* passes the summit in charge of 4M74, Mossend - Wembley 'Intermodal'; note the up and down passenger loops. (MB 5/99)

	[Level]	1 in 152	1 in 142	1 in 240
				800 ft.–
				600–
				400–
				200–

(site of
Elvanfoot
station,
closed 1965)

(site of
Crawford
station,
closed 1965)

51	Milepost mileage	52		53		54		55
350		351		352		353	miles from London	354

ELVANFOOT : The WCML passes over the infant river Clyde near Elvanfoot, where a pair of Class 37s Nos. 37156+37051 *Merehead* are seen heading south with an MGR train of Scottish opencast coal from Mossend to Drax Power Station in Yorkshire.(BA 8/97)

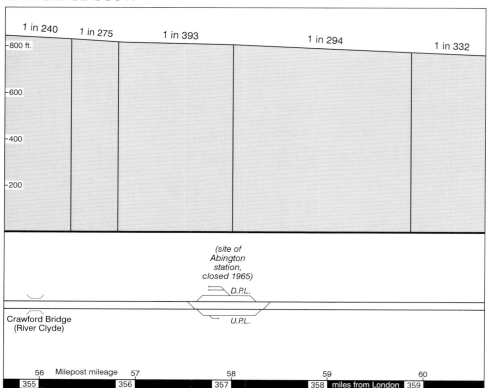

1 in 240 1 in 275 1 in 393 1 in 294 1 in 332

-800 ft.

-600

-400

-200

(site of
Abington
station,
closed 1965)

D.P.L.

Crawford Bridge
(River Clyde)

U.P.L.

56 Milepost mileage 57 58 59 60

355 356 357 358 miles from London 359

ABINGTON : Just 8 miles north of Beattock Summit there are another set of passenger loops at Abington where, sporting diiferent corporate liveries, a pair of Class 86s are seen passing on 4L60, Coatbridge - Fleixstowe freightliner. The leading locomotive is No. 86638 and White Hill provides the backdrop. (MR 5/99)

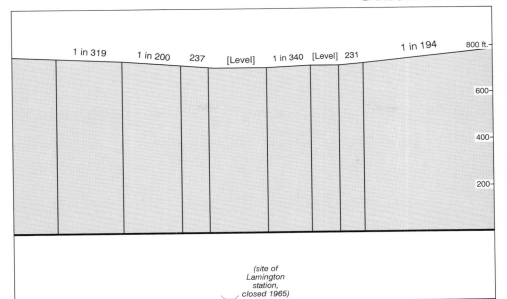

| 1 in 319 | 1 in 200 | 237 | [Level] | 1 in 340 | [Level] | 231 | 1 in 194 | 800 ft. |

600—

400—

200—

(site of
Lamington
station,
closed 1965)

Lamington Viaduct
(River Clyde)

| 61 | Milepost mileage | 62 | | 63 | | 64 | | 65 |
| 360 | | 361 | | 362 | | 363 | miles from London | 364 |

LAMINGTON : An unidentified Class 90 heads north with 1S75, the 1235 Euston - Glasgow, amidst pine-clad hills which typify the scenery in this part of the Clyde valley. (MB 5/99)

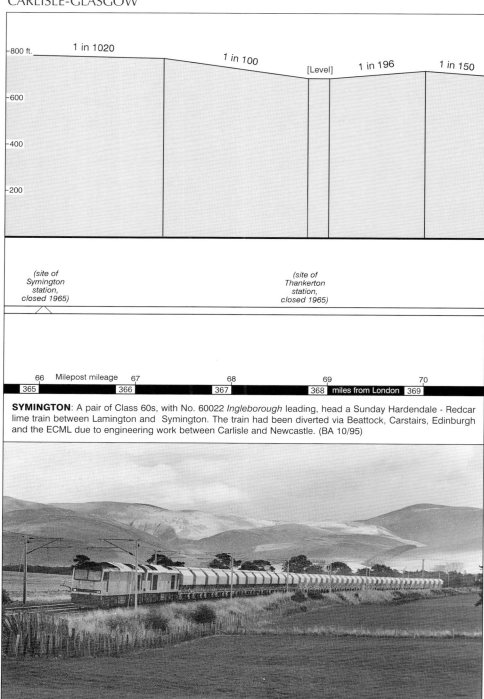

800 ft.

1 in 1020

1 in 100

[Level]

1 in 196

1 in 150

600

400

200

*(site of
Symington
station,
closed 1965)*

*(site of
Thankerton
station,
closed 1965)*

66   Milepost mileage   67   68   69   70

365   366   367   368 miles from London 369

SYMINGTON: A pair of Class 60s, with No. 60022 *Ingleborough* leading, head a Sunday Hardendale - Redcar lime train between Lamington and Symington. The train had been diverted via Beattock, Carstairs, Edinburgh and the ECML due to engineering work between Carlisle and Newcastle. (BA 10/95)

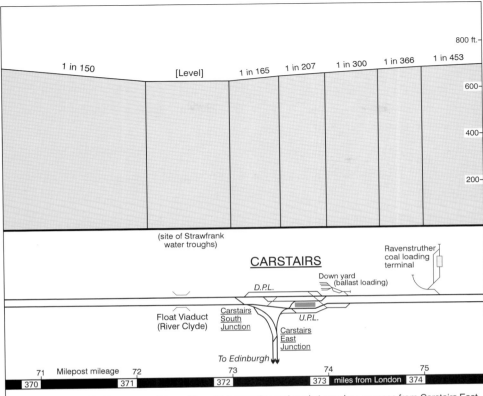

800 ft.

1 in 150   [Level]   1 in 165   1 in 207   1 in 300   1 in 366   1 in 453

600

400

200

(site of Strawfrank water troughs)

CARSTAIRS

Ravenstruther coal loading terminal

D.P.L.

Down yard (ballast loading)

Float Viaduct (River Clyde)

Carstairs South Junction

U.P.L.

Carstairs East Junction

To Edinburgh

| 71 | Milepost mileage | 72 | 73 | | 74 | | 75 |
| 370 | | 371 | 372 | | 373 | miles from London | 374 |

CARSTAIRS : A GNER set, comprising a Class 91 locomotive and mark 4 coaches, crosses from Carstairs East Junction onto the down platform line at Carstairs station with 1S21, the 1100 Kings Cross - Glasgow. The down main and down loop are visible in the foreground. (BA 9/99)

107

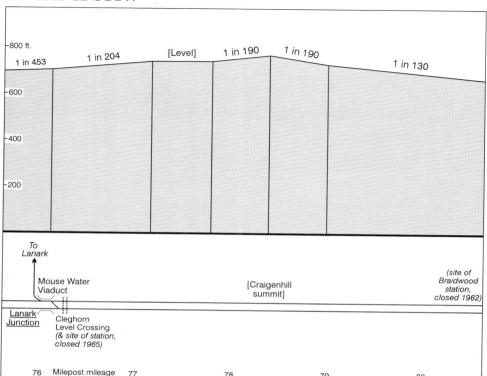

- 800 ft.

1 in 453   1 in 204   [Level]   1 in 190   1 in 190   1 in 130

- 600

- 400

- 200

To
Lanark

Mouse Water
Viaduct

[Craigenhill
summit]

(site of
Braidwood
station,
closed 1962)

Lanark
Junction

Cleghorn
Level Crossing
(& site of station,
closed 1965)

| 76 | Milepost mileage | 77 | | 78 | | 79 | | 80 |
| 375 | | 376 | | 377 | | 378 | miles from London | 379 |

CRAIGENHILL SUMMIT : This impressive shot has been published before but no apology is made for doing so again. A 400mm lens captures Class 56 No. 56093 *The Institution of Mining Engineers* using every ounce of available horsepower to lift 6L80, Deanside - Wisbech petfood service, up the climb from Law Junction to Craigenhill summit. (BA 2/96)

CARTLAND : The black and orange Loadhaul livery looks especially striking on a Class 37. Sporting this livery, No. 37713 is seen with a sister locomotive, near Cartland village, working a Mossend - Drax MGR coal train. According to the photographer, the sound was incredible! (BA 6/97)

BRAIDWOOD : Enthusiasts crane their necks out of the carriage windows to sample the 'thrash' of Class 31 No. 31465 leading a sister engine on the climb to Craigenhill Summit. The location is Braidwood and the train is the return "39 Steps" charter from Stranraer to Preston. (BA 9/97)

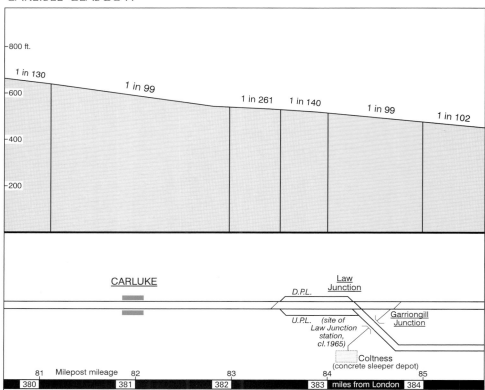

-800 ft.

1 in 130

1 in 99

-600

1 in 261   1 in 140

1 in 99

1 in 102

-400

-200

CARLUKE

Law
Junction

D.P.L.

U.P.L.   (site of
Law Junction
station,
cl.1965)

Garriongill
Junction

Coltness
(concrete sleeper depot)

81   Milepost mileage   82   83   84   85
380   381   382   383   miles from London   384

LAW JUNCTION : Res liveried Class 47 No. 47743 heads 7 vans on the 1405 Glasgow - Edinburgh - Kings Cross postal at Law Junction, which is where the Wishaw loop rejoins the WCML after leaving the main line at Shieldmuir North Junction. (BA 10/94)

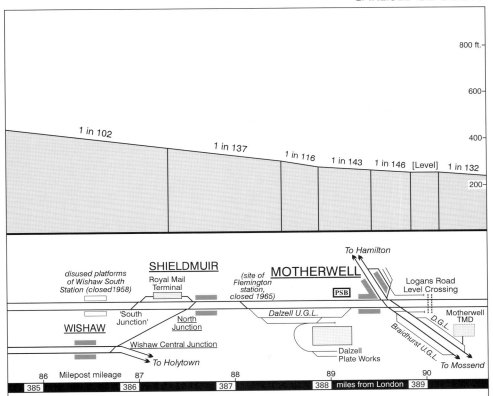

800 ft.-

600-

1 in 102

400-

1 in 137

1 in 116   1 in 143   1 in 146 [Level] 1 in 132

200-

To Hamilton

SHIELDMUIR

disused platforms
of Wishaw South
Station (closed 1958)

Royal Mail
Terminal

(site of
Flemington
station,
closed 1965)

MOTHERWELL

PSB

Logans Road
Level Crossing

'South
Junction'

North
Junction

Dalzell U.G.L.

Braidhurst U.G.L.

D.G.L.

Motherwell
TMD

WISHAW

Wishaw Central Junction

To Holytown

Dalzell
Plate Works

To Mossend

| 86 | Milepost mileage | 87 | | 88 | | 89 | | 90 |
| 385 | | 386 | | 387 | | 388 | miles from London | 389 |

SHIELDMUIR : The British Steel plant at Dalzell is located on the up side of the WCML between Motherwell and Shieldmuir. Shortly after departure, Class 60 No. 60030 *Cir Mhor* passes through Shieldmuir station with 6E30, Dalzell - Lackenby (Teeside) steel empties. (RB 4/98)

111

MOTHERWELL : Class 325 mail unit No. 325009 (above) passes Motherwell Signalling Centre; commissioned in two stages during 1972-73 and controls the WCML northwards from Kirkpatrick to milepost 98 between Newton and Rutherglen. (BA 2/99)

A panoramic view of the south end of Motherwell station shows Class 56 No. 56130 (below) heading 6L80, Deanside - Wisbech petfood train, formed of VGA vans. (RB 3/98)

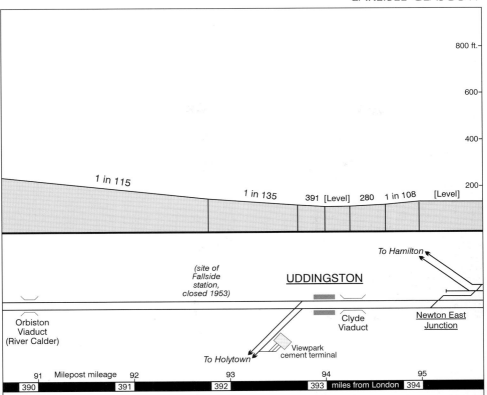

1 in 115

1 in 135   391 [Level]   280   1 in 108   [Level]

800 ft.
600
400
200

To Hamilton

(site of
Fallside
station,
closed 1953)

UDDINGSTON

Orbiston
Viaduct
(River Calder)

Clyde
Viaduct

Newton East
Junction

To Holytown

Viewpark
cement terminal

| 91 | Milepost mileage | 92 | | 93 | | 94 | | 95 |
| 390 | | 391 | | 392 | | 393 | miles from London | 394 |

NEWTON : Reminiscent of a previous era, a pair of Class 50s, Nos. D433+D400, storm through Newton with the "Midland Scotsman" charter from Birmingham to Glasgow. A Class 303 unit is stabled in the turnback siding in the background and the 'Hamilton Loop' line veers off to the right. (BA 2/94)

CARLISLE-GLASGOW

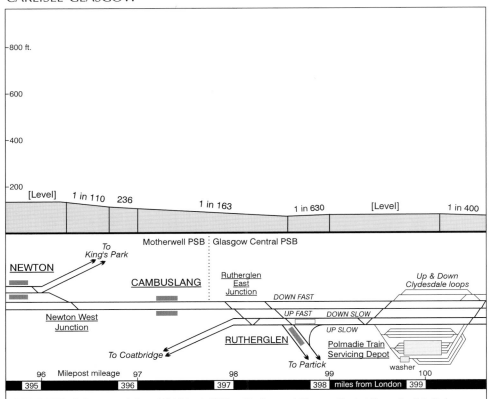

POLMADIE : Before completion of Shieldmuir RMT, mail trains used Glasgow Central. Two miles into its journey, Class 325 unit No. 325008 *Peter Howarth CBE* passes the carriage sidings at Polmadie with 1M90, Glasgow - Crewe mail. The site of Polmadie down yard is to the left of the picture. (RR 12/96)

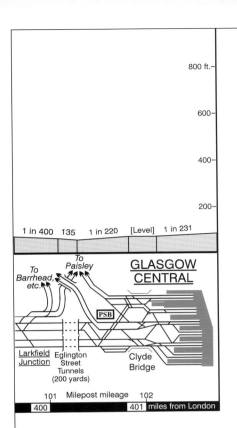

800 ft.–
600–
400–
200–

1 in 400   135   1 in 220   [Level]   1 in 231

To Paisley
To Barrhead, etc.

GLASGOW CENTRAL

PSB

Larkfield Junction   Eglington Street Tunnels (200 yards)   Clyde Bridge

101   Milepost mileage   102

400   401 miles from London

Welcome to **Glasgow Central**

GLASGOW CENTRAL : Looking south, the running lines begin to converge as a Class 101 unit, No. 101695 (above), enters the station with a service from Paisley Canal. Note the signal gantry which carries the famous 20mph speed restriction signs. (MB 7/99)

Journey's end, or perhaps the beginning! .... A local EMU service (below) leaves the terminus passing between Class 86 No. 86248 *Sir Clwyd/County of Clywd* at the head of 1O16, the 1230 Glasgow - Poole service and DVT No. 82216 on the twelve o'clock GNER service to London Kings Cross - the "Flying Scotsman". (MB 7/99)

Gallery

GALLERY

There are many locations on the WCML which afford excellent photographic opportunities; Weedon, Mill Meece or Winwick readily spring to mind, not to mention some stations, like Carlisle for example - you will have your own particular favourite(s) and many may have been illustrated already.

In this chapter of LINE BY LINE we feature some of the most popular, perhaps classic, photographic locations and have selected material which best illustrates them; the northern stretches of the WCML involving the climbs to Shap and Beattock.

These locations have stood the test of time, although there is no longer the splendour of a smoky exhaust from a steam engine hammering up the grade at speeds seldom more than 40mph. However, a different challenge presents itself today as photographers grapple to capture the majesty of windswept fells and river valleys as the WCML threads a path amidst the unsightly paraphernalia of overhead electrification wires and masts.

The colour reproductions are backed up by extracts of Ordnance Survey *Landranger* maps, with the number of each photograph overprinted on it to show where the train was captured on film. The maps and photographs will help readers familiarise themselves with the locations and, hopefully, enable new photographic opportunities to be discovered. For ease of reference, the photographs can be categorised into the following geographical areas:

Page(s)	Photograph Number	Area
119 & 120	1 to 4	Grayrigg
121 & 122	5 to 8	Lune Gorge
123 to 125	9 to 14	Shap
128	15 to 16	Beattock
129 to 132	17 to 24	Upper Clyde Valley

The extracts are kindly reproduced from *Landranger* 1 : 50 000 scale Ordnance Survey maps by permission of Ordnance Survey on behalf of the Controller of Her Majesty's Stationary Office, © Crown Copyright MC0100028152:

Sheet Number	Landranger Map Title	Date
97	Kendal & Morecambe	1998
91	Appleby-in-Westmorland	1996
90	Penrith & Keswick	1997
78	Nithsdale	1995
72	Upper Clyde Valley	1997

① **DOCKER** : Class 86 No. 86236 *Josiah Wedgewood* heads 1O38, the 0910 Edinburgh - Bournemouth, *Virgin Trains* service towards Docker, with snow-clad fells dominating the background. (DM 1/99)

② **BECK FOOT**: The up "Devon Scot", 1V57, 0910 Aberdeen - Plymouth, sweeps underneath the roadbridge which links Beck Foot and Grayrigg Head with power car No. 43153 *THE ENGLISH RIVIERA TORQUAY* leading. Note both the seasonal contrast in fauna, and the apparent variation in *Virgin* red livery, compared to the illustration on pages 120. (DM 7/97)

③ **BECK FOOT** : The M6 motorway can be glimpsed running adjacent to the main line directly above the last hopper wagon in the consist of 7L12, a Shap - Carnforth ballast, trundling past Beck Foot behind 'Mainline' liveried Class 37 No. 37371. (PJR 4/97)

④ **LOW GILL** : HST power car No. 43068 *The Red Nose* (No. 43063 at the rear) heads 1V52, the 0850 Edinburgh - Penzance "Cornish Scot", amidst the desolate fells at Low Gill. The Virgin trains livery is a delightful improvement on the old *Inter City* colours (PJR 4/97)

⑤ **DILLICAR** : A magnificent view of Class 60 No. 60098 Charles *Francis Brush* (above) rounding the foot of the Common heading an MGR train of Scottish coal bound for Fiddlers Ferry power station. (DM 7/97)

⑥ Arguably the best vista to illustrate the epic scenery of the Lune Gorge. The River Lune meanders below the WCML as Class 37 No. 37057 *Viking* (below) heads from Workington to Bescot, with a train of 300 yard lengths of continuous welded rail. (PJR 9/97)

(7) **LOW BORROWBRIDGE** : Photographed from a lay-by on the A685 Tebay to Kendal road, Class 56 No. 56119 (above) on 6V23, Hardendale - Margam lime train meets Class 60, No. 60022 heading a rake of empty HEAs from Blackburn to Ayr. (MR 4/98)

(8) A stretch of level track runs for 1½ miles just south of Tebay, site of the 'Dillicar' water troughs, where steam engines and the early diesel locomotives used to replenish their water supply. The mass of Birk Knott Fell forms the backdrop as Class 60 No. 60018 (below) heads towards Tebay on 6E48, Stanlow - Jarrow petroleum tanks; a train sadly no longer running. (PJR 5/97)

⑨ **GREENHOLME** : Photographing northbound services at Greenholme is only practical from mid-afternoon onwards when the sun is in a favourable position. Here, at 2115hrs, the shadows creep up on Class 86 No. 86241 *Glenfiddich* (above) as it lifts 1S81, Tonbridge - Glasgow mail up Shap bank. (DM 6/95)

⑩ Looking in the opposite direction, Class 90 No. 90133 (below) makes its descent from Shap in heather clad Orton Moor cutting with the southbound 6G90, Carlisle Yard- Bescot 'Enterprise' service. (DM 8/98)

⑪ **SCOUT GREEN** : A Cricklewood - Penrith 'Milkliner' operated for a trial 4 week period in 1997 and is seen being hauled by a pair of DRS Class 20s, Nos. 20303+20304 (above) at Scout Green; some 40 years span the design of the Class 20 locomotive and the Class 92 featured on page 129. (DM 7/97)

⑫ The desolate Westmorland countryside around Shap Wells is perfectly captured in this panoramic view of Class 86 No. 86212 *Preston Guild* 1328-1992 (below) seen in charge of the 0625 Manchester - Glasgow, some 3 miles from the summit. (DM 4/94)

(13) **BESSIE GHYLL** : The sinuous section of the WCML north of Shap between Thrimby Grange and Bessie Ghyll (sometimes known as Great Strickland but not by railwaymen) presents the photographer with a contrasting and delightful panorama. Amidst the pine trees in Sheriff park is Class 60 No. 60061 *Alexander Graham Bell* (above) on 7M30, Knockshinnoch - Fiddlers Ferry MGR coal train. (PJR 9/97)

(14) A few hundred yards to the North, as the line wends its way through the wooded ravine which carries the infant River Leith, Class 87 No. 87015 *Howard of Effingham* (below) emerges from a cutting onto an embankment in charge of 1S83, the 1440 Euston - Glasgow. (PJR 4/97)

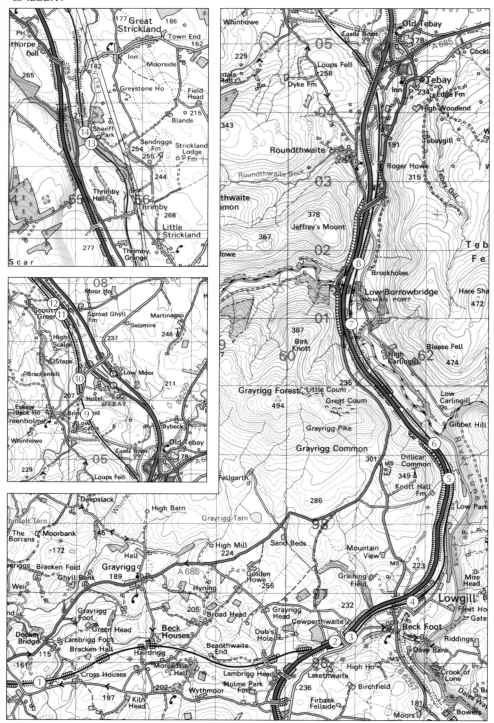

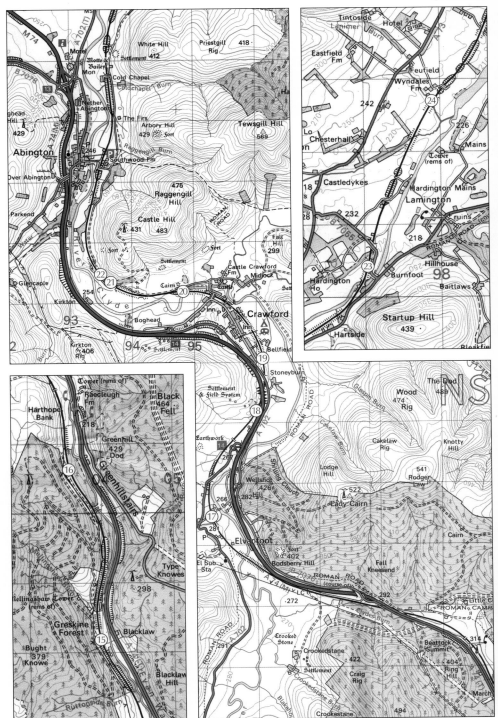

(15) **GRESKINE** : As we went to press, an updated *Landranger* map had not been published to show the new motorway over Beattock. Following the contour of the new road, a pair of Class 86 locomotives Nos. 86607 *The Institution of Electrical Engineers* + 86606 descend Beattock bank at Greskine hauling 4L60, Coatbridge - Felixstowe freightliner. (MB 7/99)

(16) **HARTHOPE** : Scenic Harthope Bank, 5 miles from Beattock summit, is the setting for Class 86 No. 86419 *Post Haste*, in former Res livery, at the helm of the 0716 Penzance - Glasgow "Cornish Scot", at this time formed of *InterCity* Mark 2 coaches. (PJR 5/91)

17 **ELVANFOOT** : The Clitheroe - Gunnie cement train was a popular sight on the WCML as it was 'booked' for a pair of Class 37s and ran in daylight hours. Here, Nos. 37380+37370 power the train at Elvanfoot, where the WCML emerges into the Upper Clyde valley. (PJR 6/90)

18 **CRAWFORD** : The Class 92 represents the last electric locomotive to be introduced onto the rail network and one example, No. 92024 *J. S. Bach*, is seen south of Crawford heading 4S90, Wembley - Mossend 'Intermodal'; a service which conveys containers/swapbodies from mainland Europe, via the Channel Tunnel to Scotland. (PJR 9/98)

GALLERY

19 **CRAWFORD** : Photographic opportunities are plentiful amidst the Lowther Hills of South Lanarkshire. The 'T' shaped plantation of coniferous pine on Tewsgill Hill, provides a distinctive backdrop for 'Mainline' liveried Class 37s Nos. 37023+37379 (above) seen heading a lengthy 6L80, Deanside - Wisbech petfood train, on the climb to Beattock. (BA 5/97)

20 Class 90 No. 90004 (below) propels the 1340 Glasgow - Euston across the River Clyde and heads towards the village of Crawford, which can be glimpsed to the far right of the picture. (PJR 11/95)

㉑ **ABINGTON** : These two photographs illustrate the same location but show how differing elevations and focal lengths provide contrasting perspectives. Class 92 No. 92025 *Oscar Wilde* (above) sweeps round Castle Hill with 4M74, Mossend - Wembley 'Intermodal'. (MB 7/99)

㉒ Whilst a more panoramic view sees Class 86 No. 86425 (below) hauling the longest passenger service in the country, the 0900 Aberdeen - Plymouth "Devon Scot". (PJR 5/91)

(23) **LAMINGTON** : Photographed from the B7055 road, Class 60 No. 60055 *Thomas Barnardo* (above) approaches Lamington with 6S36, Dalston - Grangemouth tanks, some still distinguishable in the distinctive British Petroleum green livery. (BA 6/97)

(24) A profusion of brightly coloured deep-sea containers greet the cameraman near Wyndales Farm, mid-way between Lamington and Symington, as an unidentified Class 90 (below) proceeds northwards with 4S87, Felixstowe - Coatbridge freightliner. (BA 6/96)

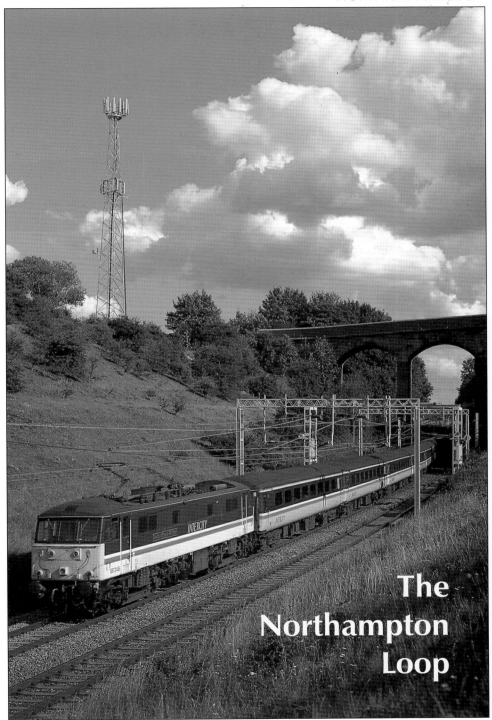

The Northampton Loop

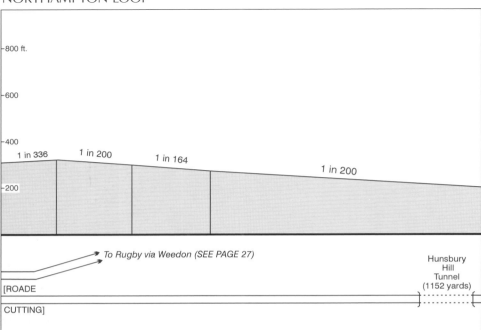

800 ft.

600

400

1 in 336   1 in 200   1 in 164   1 in 200

200

To Rugby via Weedon (SEE PAGE 27)

Hunsbury
Hill
Tunnel
(1152 yards)

[ROADE

CUTTING]

| 60 | | 61 | | 62 | | 63 | miles from London | 64 |

COURTENHALL : Resplendent in RfD livery, Class 47 No. 47293 enters Courtenhall Cutting near Roade on the 28¼ mile long Northampton Loop with 4A36, Lawley Street – Wembley 'Intermodal' service. (AG 5/97)

HUNSBURY HILL TUNNEL : Mainline blue liveried Class 37 No. 37371 emerges from Hunsbury Hill Tunnel with a spoil train bound for Forders tip, near Bedford. (AG 5/97)

NORTHAMPTON : A sylvan scene of Class 90 No.90029 *Frachtverbindungen* crossing the River Nene at '15 Arches', Northampton, with 6S48, Dagenham – Mossend train of Ford vehicles. The locomotive carries the unique German Federal Railways red and white livery. (AG 5/98)

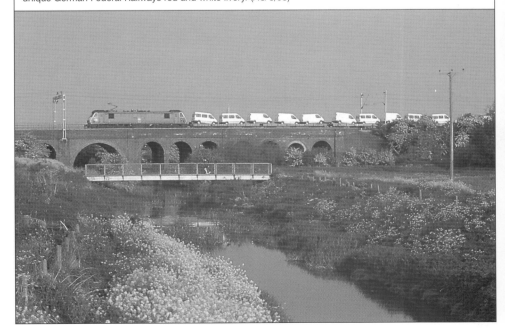

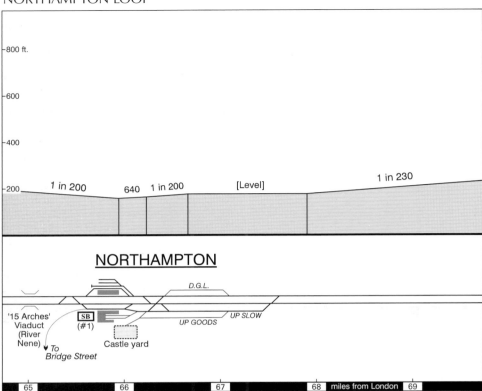

-800 ft.

-600

-400

-200
1 in 200   640   1 in 200   [Level]   1 in 230

NORTHAMPTON

D.G.L.

'15 Arches'
Viaduct
(River
Nene)   SB
(#1)   UP GOODS   UP SLOW

Castle yard

→ To
Bridge Street

| 65 | 66 | 67 | 68 miles from London | 69 |

NORTHAMPTON : Class 90 No. 90014 heads 1H10, the diverted 1050 Euston – Manchester, through Northampton station and passes light engines Nos. 92008+90137 on the bi-directional up/slow line. (AG 5/98)

NORTHAMPTON : A pair of Class 47s Nos. 47236 *Rover Group Quality Assured* +47312 *Parsec of Europe* (above) pass Northampton No. 1 signalbox with 4P12, Wembley – Hams Hall 'Intermodal'. The spur descending from the mainline leads to Bridge Street. (AG 5/98)

Once the Tinsley flagship, Class 47 No. 47145 *Merriden Emrys* (below) leads sister Class 47, No. 47228, past the site of Northampton No 3 signalbox in charge of 6G90, Wembley – Washwood Heath 'Connectrail' service. Behind are Northampton up sidings which have previously been used for stabling 'Cobbler' ECS, 321/4s and infrastructure trains. (AG 6/96)

-800 ft.

-600

-400

1 in 230

-200

(site of
Church Brampton
station,
closed 1931)

(site of
Althorp Park
station,
closed 1960)

| 70 | | 71 | | 72 | | 73 | miles from London | 74 |

BRINGTON : Class 319 unit No. 319001 heads the Connex South Central 1242 Rugby – Gatwick Airport service on the up line at Brington . (KF 8/98)

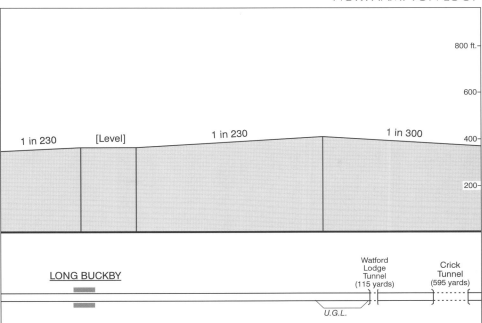

800 ft.-

600-

1 in 230   [Level]   1 in 230   1 in 300   400-

200-

LONG BUCKBY

Watford
Lodge
Tunnel
(115 yards)

Crick
Tunnel
(595 yards)

U.G.L.

75   76   77   78   miles from London   79

LONG BUCKBY : Awaiting departure time at Long Buckby is Class 321 unit No. 321429 with a 'Silverlink' service to London Euston; Long Buckby being the last station on the Northampton Loop before the WCML is joined once again at Rugby. (MB 7/99)

WATFORD LODGE : Watford Lodge loop and tunnel are both visible in this composition of Class 321 unit No. 321436 in charge of the 0916 Rugby – Euston. (KF 5/98)

CRICK : Class 90 No. 90005 passes over the crossover which serves as the entry into the southern end of DIRFT and approaches Crick Tunnel with a diverted Manchester – Euston service. (AG 6/97)

DIRFT : or, DRIFT, is commonly used to describe Daventry International Railfreight Terminal; opened in May 1997 and situated 3 miles east of Rugby on the north side of the Northampton Loop adjacent to Jct. 18 of the M1. SNCF liveried Class 90 No. 90130 *Fretconnection* (above) leaves the terminal having called with 4A11, Trafford Park – Wembley 'Intermodal' service. (AG 7/97)

Class 86 No. 86207 *City of Lichfield* (below) passes the very securely fenced sidings of DIRFT propelling 1A71, the diverted 1719 Wolverhampton – Euston. (AG 7/97)

800 ft.

600

400

1 in 300

200

*(site of
Kilsby & Crick
station,
closed 1960)*

<u>Rugby
South
Junction</u>

Daventry International
RailFreight Terminal
(DIRFT)

*[continued
on page 31]*

| 80 | 81 | 82 | 83 | miles from London | 84 |

NORTOFT LANE : The final (sectional) photograph, fittingly features the latest locomotive class to see service on the WCML – the Class 66. With the famous Rugby masts, built in 1937, filling the sky, No. 66026 passes Nortoft Lane with 4A36, Hams Hall – Wembley 'Intermodal'. (MB 7/99)

Glossary

Miles & Chains

These tables set out the WCML mileage in the down direction from London Euston to Glasgow Central, plus the Northampton Loop.

Cumulative Mileage is the Miles and Chains (M.Ch.) sequentially from Euston (0.00) through to Glasgow Central (401.35) and **Local Mileage** indicates when cumulative mileposts are replaced by local mileposts besides the running lines. Every station, junction, tunnel and goods loop on the route is listed under **Location**; stations are highlighted in bold typeface and the **Page Number** of the corresponding schematic map is given for cross reference purposes.

Cumulative Mileage	Local Mileage	Location	Page Number
(M. Ch)	(M. Ch)		
0. 00		**LONDON EUSTON**	10
1. 36		*Camden Junction*	
1. 54		*Primrose Hill Tunnels (east portals)*	
2. 27		*Primrose Hill Tunnels (west portals)*	
4. 45		*Kensal Green Tunnels (east portals)*	
4. 59		*Kensal Green Tunnels (west portals)*	
5. 23		*West London Junction*	
5. 65		*Willesden Junction*	
8. 04		**Wembley Central**	12
11. 30		**Harrow & Wealdstone**	14
15. 79		**Bushey**	15
17. 35		**Watford Junction**	15
18. 33		*Watford Tunnel Slow Line (south portal)*	
18. 38		*Watford Tunnel Fast Line (south portal)*	
19. 40		*Watford Tunnels (north portals)*	
20. 74		**Kings Langley**	16
23. 06		**Apsley**	16
24. 39		**Hemel Hempstead**	16
27. 75		**Berkhamsted**	17
31. 53		**Tring**	18
36. 08		**Cheddington**	19
40. 14		**Leighton Buzzard**	20
46. 46		**Bletchley**	22
49. 65		**MILTON KEYNES**	23
52. 33		**Wolverton**	23
56. 47		*Hanslope Junction*	
68. 09		*Stowe Hill Tunnel (south portal)*	
68. 32		*Stowe Hill Tunnel (north portal)*	
76. 64		*Kilsby Tunnel (south portal)*	
78. 13		*Kilsby Tunnel (north portal)*	
82. 26		*Rugby South Junction*	
82. 40		**RUGBY**	31
83. 18		*Trent Valley Junction*	
96. 61 / 68		*Nuneaton South Junction*	
97. 10		**NUNEATON**	36

(M. Ch)	(M. Ch)	Location	Page
97. 36		*Nuneaton North Junction*	
102. 17		**Atherstone**	37
106. 37		**Polesworth**	38
110. 12		**TAMWORTH LOW LEVEL**	39
116. 23		**Lichfield Trent Valley**	40
116. 28		*High Level Goods Loop Junction*	
124. 22		**Rugeley**	41
124. 39		*Rugeley North Junction*	
127. 08		*Colwich Junction*	
133. 04		*Trent Valley Junction No. 1*	
133. 43		**STAFFORD**	43
138. 72		**Norton Bridge**	45
139. 00		*Norton Bridge North Junction*	
149. 74		*Madeley Junction*	
156. 16		*Basford Hall Junction*	
157. 60		*Crewe South Junction*	
158. 00		**CREWE**	49
158. 13 / 16		*Crewe North Junction*	
158. 58		*Coal Yard Junction*	
165. 41		**Winsford**	53
169. 64		**Hartford**	53
170. 55		*Hartford L.N.W. Junction*	
172. 38		**Acton Bridge**	54
174. 22		*Weaver Junction (Up Line)*	
175. 20		*Weaver Junction (Down Line)*	
180. 24		*Acton Grange Junction*	
181. 76		*Warrington South Junction*	
182. 11		**WARRINGTON BANK QUAY**	56
183. 40		*Warrington RMT*	
185. 49		*Winwick Junction*	
	(0. 00)	*(Parkside West Junction)*	
187. 77	0. 53	*Golborne Junction*	
189. 66	2. 42	*Haydock Branch Junction*	
191. 67	4. 43	*Bamfurlong Sidings Junction*	
192. 42	5. 18	*Springs Branch Junction*	
193. 57	6. 33	*Wigan Station Junction*	
193. 71	6. 47	**WIGAN NORTH WESTERN**	61
201. 42	14. 18	*Balshaw Lane Junction*	
202. 27	15. 03	**Euxton Balshaw Lane**	64
203. 45	16. 21	*Euxton Junction*	
204. 78	17. 54	**Leyland**	65
206. 21	18. 77	*Farington Junction*	
207. 32	20. 08	*Farington Curve junction*	
209. 01	21. 57 / 0.00	**PRESTON**	65
209. 34	0. 33	*Fylde Junction*	
210. 73	1. 72	*Oxheys Up Goods Loop*	
213. 26	4. 25	*Barton & Broughton Down Passing Loop*	
226. 79	17. 78	*Oubeck Up/Down Goods Loops*	
229. 79	20. 78 / 0. 00	**LANCASTER**	72

GLOSSARY

(M. Ch)	(M. Ch)	Location	Page
231. 71	1. 72	*Morecambe South Junction*	
233. 09	3. 10	*Hest Bank*	
236. 07	6. 08	*Carnforth North Junction*	
248. 64	18. 65	*Oxenholme Goods Loops*	
249. 07	19. 08	**OXENHOLME**	76
256. 18	26. 19	*Grayrigg Up/Down Goods Loops*	
261. 78	31. 79	*Tebay Up/Down Goods Loops*	
267. 67	37. 68	**SHAP SUMMIT**	
269. 08	39. 09	*Hardendale Quarry (Shap)*	
271. 37	41. 38	*Harrisons Sidings Down Goods Loop*	
277. 50	47. 51	*Eden Valley Up Goods Loop*	
281. 19	51. 20	**PENRITH**	86
286. 20	56. 21	*Plumpton Up Goods Loop*	
297. 58	67. 59	*Upperby Bridge Junction*	
299. 08	69. 09 / 0.00	**CARLISLE CITADEL**	89
301. 07	1. 79	*Kingmoor*	
306. 35	7. 27	*Admiralty Sidings Junction*	
306. 72	7. 64	*Mossband Junction*	
307. 65	8. 57	*Gretna Junction*	
309. 21	10. 13	*Quintinshill Up/Down Goods Loops*	
324. 74	25. 66	**LOCKERBIE**	98
338. 70	39. 62	*Beattock Up/Down Goods Loops*	
348. 72	49. 64	**BEATTOCK SUMMIT**	
356. 78	57. 70	*Abington Up/Down Goods Loops*	
372. 21	73. 13	*Carstairs South Junction*	
372. 61	73. 53	**CARSTAIRS**	107
375. 16	76. 08	*Lanark Junction*	
381. 03	81. 75	**Carluke**	110
383. 17	84. 09	*Law Junction*	
383. 67	84. 59	*Garriongill Junction*	
386. 34	87. 26	*Shieldmuir RMT*	
386. 47	87. 39	*Shieldmuir North Junction*	
386. 67	87. 59	**Shieldmuir**	111
388. 46	89. 38	**MOTHERWELL**	111
392. 63	93. 55	*Uddingston Junction*	
393. 00	93. 72	**Uddingston**	113
394. 23	95. 15	*Newton East Junction*	
394. 65	95. 57	**(Newton)**	114
395. 32	96. 24	*Newton West Junction*	
396. 32	97. 24	**Cambuslang**	114
397. 40	98. 32	*Rutherglen East Junction*	
398. 05	98. 77	*Rutherglen Central Junction*	
398. 28	99. 20	*Rutherglen West Junction*	
399. 23	100. 15	*Polmadie*	
400. 09	101. 01	*Larkfield Junction*	
400. 47	101. 39	*Eglington Street Junction*	
400. 64	101. 56	*Bridge Steet Junction*	
401. 35	102. 27	**GLASGOW CENTRAL**	115

NORTHAMPTON LOOP

(M. Ch)	(M. Ch)	Location	Page
56. 47		*Hanslope Junction*	
64. 00		*Hunsbury Hill Tunnel (south portal)*	
64. 53		*Hunsbury Hill Tunnel (north portal)*	
65. 58		**Northampton**	**136**
75. 37		**Long Buckby**	**139**
78. 28		*Watford Lodge Up/Down Goods Loops*	
78. 50		*Watford Lodge Tunnel (south portal)*	
78. 55		*Watford Lodge Tunnel (north portal)*	
79. 20		*Crick Tunnel (south portal)*	
79. 47		*Crick Tunnel (north portal)*	
84. 53		*Rugby South Junction*	
84. 67		**RUGBY**	**31**

Notes:

1. 80 chains = 1 Mile.

2. Mileposts occur every ¼ mile.

3. All so called 'Junctions' which only exist as a crossover or where the number of running lines change (ie. 2 to 4 track and vice-versa) are excluded from all the above tables.

4. The Miles and Chains shown for a Goods Loop, is the mid-point mileage in all instances.

Photographers

The photographers enlisted to contribute material for this edition of LINE BY LINE are named below along with a note of their initials, used for reference purposes in the captions.

Bob Avery	(BA)	Antony Guppy	(AG)	Brian Morrison	(BM)
Brian Beer	(BB)	Brian Hughes	(BH)	Peter J Robinson	(PJR)
Hugh Ballantyne	(HB)	Dave McAlone	(DM)	Alan Sherratt	(AS)
Keith Francis	(KF)				

Supplementary material:	Martin Buck	(MB)	Mark Rawlinson	(MR)
	Robert Brown	(RB)	Robin Ralston	(RR)

Brief details of other illustrations in the book are as follows:

Page	Location	Description	By
5	Cheddington	47258 : 4M54, 1235 Purfleet - Crewe	MB (6/99)
6	Hartford Jct.	90029 : 6L48, 1920 Halewood - Dagenham	MR (7/97)
9	Rugby	87015 : 1G33, 1545 Euston - Wolverhampton	MB (8/99)
33	Stafford	47287 : 4O27, 0500 Coatbridge - Southampton	MB (9/99)
67	Greenholme	87034 : 1S83, 1435 Euston - Glasgow	MB (7/99)
91	Lamington	HST : 1S71, 0720 Penzance - Glasgow	MB (5/99)
115	Glasgow	"Welcome to Glasgow Central" sign sited on PSB	MB (7/99)
117	Greenholme	90126 : 4M74, 1440 Mossend - Wembley	MB (4/97)
133	Courteenhall	86248 : 1A65, 1619 Wolverhampton - Euston	AG (7/97)
143	Winwick Jct.	37074 : 6G85, 1047 Workington - Bescot	MB (4/97)
147	Carlisle	Citadel station 150 years commemorative mural	MB (8/99)
147	Beattock	Beattock Summit Board (1,016 feet)	MB (7/99)

Bibliography

Gradient Profiles:	Ian Allan Ltd, Undated	ISBN 0-7110-0875-2
Mile By Mile:	David Maxey, 1987	ISBN 0-906025-44-3
British Rail track Diagrams:	Quail Map Company, 1990	ISBN 0-900609-74-5
Railway Track Diagrams:	Quail Map Company, 1993	ISBN 0-900609-95-8
Rail Atlas (GB & Ireland):	Stuart Baker, 1996	ISBN 0-86093-534-5
Rail Centres: Carlisle:	Peter W Robinson, 1986	ISBN 0-7110-1429-9
Modern Railways:	Ian Allan Ltd, various dates	